SALT-WATER TRINNIES

IMMIGRANT COMMUNITIES & ETHNIC MINORITIES IN THE UNITED STATES & CANADA: NO. 73

Series Editor: Robert J. Theodoratus
Department of Anthropology, Colorado State University

Continued at back of book

SALT-WATER TRINNIES:
Afro-Trinidadian Immigrant Networks and Non-Assimilation in Los Angeles

Christine Ho

AMS Press
New York

Library of Congress Cataloging-in-Publication Data

Ho, Christine G. T., 1943–
    Salt-water trinnies : Afro-Trinidadian immigrant networks and non-assimilation in Los Angeles / by Christine Ho.
      (Immigrant communities & ethnic minorities in the United States & Canada ; 73)
    Includes bibliographical references (p.) and index.
    ISBN 0-404-19483-4
    1. West Indian Americans—California—Los Angeles—Social conditions.   2. Los Angeles (Calif.)—Social conditions.   3. Los Angeles (Calif.)—Emigration and immigration.   4. Trinidad—Emigration and immigration. I. Title. II. Series.
F870.W54H6   1991
305.868′729079494—dc20

91-2297
CIP

All AMS Books are printed on acid-free paper that meets the guidelines for performance and durability of the Committee on Production Guidelines for Book Longevity of the Council on Library Resources.

AMS Press, Inc.
56 East 13th Street
New York, N.Y. 10003

Manufactured in the United States of America

FRESH-WATER YANKEE:
A Trinidadian who spends a short time in
the U.S. and comes back home with a heavy
American accent. Originally, a person who
acquires the "Yankee" accent without
leaving freshwater (without crossing the
seas), or by simply visiting the U.S.
Embassy or the U.S. Naval Base at
Chaguaramas.

from Cote Ce, Cote La:
Trinidad and Tobago Dictionary,

by John Mendes

SALT-WATER TRINNIE:
A Trinidadian who has crossed the seas
(saltwater) by moving to the United States
and continues to cross them frequently,
considering him/herself to be Trinidadian.

Christine Ho

To Robert
with love

TABLE OF CONTENTS

LIST OF TABLES

ACKNOWLEDGEMENTS

My greatest debt is owed to the participants in this research, whose cooperation and generosity made this research possible. Words are inadequate to express my gratitude to those individuals described in this book, who willingly permitted me to intrude in their personal lives without reward and shared their time freely with me. Many thanks go to Claudette Chapman for her assistance in this research and her unflagging encouragement.

Financial support for this study was provided by a Chancellor's Patent Fund Grant from the University of California, Los Angeles. I received additional funds from a Cannonball Adderley Memorial Fellowship awarded by the Center for Afro-American Studies at the University of California, Los Angeles. I am grateful to both of these sources of funding.

My gratitude extends further to Claudia Mitchell-Kernan, for her vital support during the initial writing of this book. I must acknowledge her careful reading of chapters and comments on drafts which made the writing process more bearable.

My thanks also go out to Pierre-Michel Fontaine, who introduced me to a body of knowledge on Caribbean political economy, thereby adding a dimension to this book that would otherwise have been missing. Melvin Oliver deserves thanks for sharing with me his expertise on network analysis and for much support during trying times.

Apart from his comments on drafts of this book, my husband, Robert Edgerton, deserves special praise. The writing process has been likened to a marathon and been described as the loneliness of the long-distance writer. The solitude of the writer can only be matched by the involuntary cloisterhood endured by the spouse of said writer. To thank him for his infinite patience and faith, is to be a master of understatement.

I would also like to thank Lewis L. Langness for providing indispensable technical support for the preparation of this book and Lupe Montano who typed the originial manuscript.

INTRODUCTION

Recently, TIME Magazine (June 13, 1983:18-25) featured a cover story characterizing Los Angeles as "The New Ellis Island" which, according to a Rand Corporation demographer, had become the latest embarkation point for immigrants to the United States. Fear of multiracialism, multiculturalism and multilingualism pervaded the article which declared that "Los Angeles is being invaded" by "international hordes." Apart from its xenophobic qualities, the article is noteworthy for the conspicuous absence of any reference to the Caribbean immigrant presence in Los Angeles, even though many other immigrant groups are listed and discussed, such as Mexicans (2,100,000), Guatemalans (50,000), Salvadorans (200,000), Armenians (175,000), Iranians (200,000), Arabs (130,000), Israelis (90,000), Japanese (175,000), Chinese (153,000), Koreans (150,000), Vietnamese (40,000), Filipinos (150,000), and Samoans (60,000).

This comes as no surprise. In a seminal article published over a decade ago, Bryce-Laporte (1972) pointed out that the black immigrant experience, in essence, is one of double invisibility. By this he meant that as a black, the black immigrant suffers the sort of invisibility so poignantly depicted in Ralph

1

Ellison's novel, <u>Invisible Man</u>. At the same time, as a foreigner, the black immigrant suffers invisibility vis-a-vis the white host society. The recent article in TIME testifies to the currency of this observation.

Bryce-Laporte (1972) further observed that black immigrants, apart from being invisible to the public at large, had also escaped the scrutiny of American scholarship, including those scholars of the immigrant experience in America. At the time of Bryce-Laporte's writing, the only known work on black immigrants, apart from his own, was a study by a black sociologist, Ira de A. Reid, entitled <u>The Negro Immigrant</u>, originally published in 1939. In this work, Reid was principally concerned with the problem of social adjustment of the black immigrants to life in America, especially vis-a-vis the black American population (Reid 1968: orig. 1939).

As Reid saw it, black immigrants faced several obstacles in adjusting to life in America. First, the black immigrant was steeped in a cultural tradition quite different from that of the black American. Second, the black immigrant came from a background based on a three-tiered color-class social system, in contrast to the two-tiered racial system of the United States. Finally, the black immigrant was entering a society where his/her race was a numerical minority after having spent his/her life in societies where his/her race was a majority (Reid 1968:35).

With one or two exceptions, most of the demographic characteristics of the population studied by Reid are still valid today. In terms of age, the immigrants were mostly young: between the ages of 14 and 44 (Reid 1968:79). Men outnumbered women by 143:199 (Reid 1968:80). Most immigrants were single (Reid 1968:83). Their main occupations were either industrial workers (male) or domestics (female) (Reid 1968:83). They tended to be better educated than black Americans (Reid 1968:84) and their destinations in the United States were along the Eastern seaboard, particularly the states of New York, Massachusetts and Florida where they remained. Sixty-five percent of them lived in New York City (Reid 1968:85). Furthermore, they were concentrated in large cities and 80 percent of them were of urban origin and held urban occupations (Reid 1968:89). The Caribbean immigrant population of today deviates only slightly from this description. The sex ratio has swung to the other end of the pendulum and they are occupationally more diverse than when Reid studied them.

The void in knowledge of Caribbean immigrants is no longer as profound as it once was. However, the literature that has accumulated tends to center on Puerto Ricans, Cubans, Dominicans, and more recently, Haitians, while those from the Anglophone Caribbean remain somewhat neglected. It is hoped that this book will contribute in some small way to expanding the corpus of knowledge of immigrants from the English-speaking Caribbean.

In this book I will describe and analyze the complex phenomenon of Afro-Trinidadian immigration to the United States, and by logical extension, its regional counterpart, West Indian immigration, as a component of the New Immigration. Post-1965 immigration to the United States has been labelled New Immigration because it constitutes a radical departure from that preceding it (Bryce-Laporte 1977). In volume alone, the New Immigration has reached unprecedented levels. More importantly, however, the complexion of immigration has changed. The New Immigrants are not of European stock but are, instead, Latin American, Asian, Middle Eastern, Afro-Caribbean and even African. They are phenotypically, culturally and linguistically different from white Americans. In my view, this poses a formidable challenge to American society which will have to address the implications of multiracialism, multiculturalism and multilingualism in ways far more effectively than in the past.

The West Indian immigrant experience is distinctive in several respects. First, the migration process of the majority of West Indians is taking place at an historical moment in the post-industrial age: it is occurring during an era of mass media communications such as radio, television, satellite communications, international telephone and telex and even jet travel. The "international shuttling" made possible by jet travel invites a rethinking of the nature of migrant adaptation. Second, it has been suggested that the principle of social organization in the post-industrial age is "social and communications networks" (Richmond 1981:298-319). The context of West Indian migration is one in which social networks transcend national boundaries. These networks of kin and friends make it possible for West Indian migration to occur. They also shape patterns of migration by recruiting new migrants and by nurturing close ties to their places of origin. In effect, they encapsulate migrants in social worlds based on likeness. Third, institutionalized racism in the U.S. has had a tremendous impact on West Indian immigrants. As black immigrants, West Indians have been daily confronted with discrimination on the basis of their color and have experienced status changes along with the change in residence. The impact of this has been to bring about a shift in racial consciousness and group identity based on race.

West Indian patterns of migration and settlement defy the expectations of the assimilation paradigm. Their group orientation based on race, extended kin networks, "home boy" friendship ties and social clubs, coupled with transnational social networks and other persisting international linkages such as "shuttling," militate against their incorporation into the mainstream of American life.

CHAPTER I

RETHINKING THE ASSIMILATION OF THE NEW IMMIGRANTS

By altering the ethnic and racial composition
of the population of the United States, the New
Immigration demands a re-appraisal of the
assimilation paradigm. More specifically, I am
suggesting that West Indian immigration, if
considered as one black component of the New
Immigration to the United States, challenges any
assumptions that such assimilation is to be the
inevitable end product of immigration, as well as
calling into question any notion that integration
is an organizing principle of American society.
These are the guiding questions which form the
basis of my research, inspired by observations made
by scholars of the immigrant experience in America.
Steinberg (1981:42), for example, has noted that
the goal of assimilation in America has only been
achieved by arrivals from Europe.   Others have
observed that the stigma of non-whiteness has led
to a distinctive modus vivendi for some non-white
immigrants. Dominguez (1975) and Laguerre (1984)
both argue that a crucial element in the adaptation
of West Indian immigrants to life in America has
been the formation and maintenance of racial and
ethnic boundaries (Dominguez 1975:33; Laguerre
1984:155).
     Put differently, West Indian immigrants are
perceived by the larger society as blacks because

5

of their skin color, and they are consequently consigned to the same social status as the greater part of black Americans.   In the same way that racial minorities in America have always been subjected to segregation, the racist structure of American society often forces black immigrants to be incorporated into permanent niches in pre-existing ghettos (Laguerre 1984:156).   The systematic structural separation on the collective level that black immigrants have encountered upon their arrival in America has played a large part both in the evolution of a complex, and at times contradictory, awareness of their ethnicity, and in their grasp of the dynamics of American race relations; both of these are manifested in a powerful racial consciousness.

The goal of this book is to examine one component of the New Immigration.   More specifically, my research focuses on a sample of black immigrants from Trinidad and Tobago who are in the United States, living in Los Angeles. Utilizing social network analysis as a methodological tool, I examine their primary social relationships in Los Angeles by looking at marriage patterns, the composition and structure of their kin-based networks, and the quality of interaction with kin in Los Angeles.   I also inquire into the form and content of their friendship networks in Los Angeles, as well as their participation in voluntary associations. Most importantly, by examining the ethnic and racial composition of their friendship networks, I hope to gain insight into the process of ethnification and changes in group consciousness brought about by their immigrant experiences.   By these means, I hope to acquire knowledge of the structure of their group life within the United States and their reception in, or rejection by, American social institutions.

In addition, I will probe the transcontinental and transnational linkages that continue to bind them in various ways to the Commonwealth Caribbean. This is because their primary social relationships

extend beyond the confines of this country and
encompass networks of kin and friends dispersed
throughout the North American continent, as well
as kin and friends who have remained in the West
Indies. These kin-based and friend-based networks
criss-cross oceans and continents: their very
existence deflects energy away from strong rooting
in America. Their upkeep also detracts from
primary group relations with the Euro-American
majority. More importantly, however,
Afro-Trinidadian immigrants' cold reception within
American social institutions, most notably housing
segregation and exclusion from first-rate education
and employment, favors their structural separation.
The obstructive nature of their transnational
social networks, their insular way of life within
the United States, and their incorporation into the
black sub-society of America, combine to impede the
assimilation of Afro-Trinidadian immigrants.

THE DEVELOPMENT OF THE ASSIMILATION PARADIGM

The "melting pot" concept, which Americans have
held as an ideal throughout the history of United
States immigration, presents a view of American
life which is in contrast to that delineated above.
As a symbol, the "melting pot" ideal owed its
popularity to a liberal vision of America as a land
of opportunity where religion, race, and national
origin were deemed irrelevant to the struggle for a
better life (Hirschman 1983). The idea of
assimilation was the logical culmination of these
beliefs. The school of thought founded on these
principles also postulated that "primordial" bonds
such as race and ethnicity would decline in
significance and ultimately vanish because of the
requirements of industrialization. In a modern,
industrialized world, socio-economic rewards would
naturally be distributed on the basis of merit and
achievement rather than on sentimental and

ascriptive criteria such as race and ethnicity
(Blauner 1972:3-4).

Robert E. Park is credited with the founding of
the "Chicago School" of thought concerning race and
ethnic relations on which assimilation theory was
built.   Park was a pioneer who, in the early
decades of this century, published extensively on
early European immigrants to the United States and
on black migrants from the South to Northern
cities.   He did this at a moment in American
history when both of these population movements
were occurring on an unprecedented scale. His work
on "racial and cultural contacts" formed the
theoretical underpinnings of a model that
eventually came to dominate the study of race and
ethnicity in American social science for many
decades (Blauner 1972; Geschwender 1978; Gordon
1964; Hirschman 1983; Steinberg 1981).

Park formulated his theory of the "race
relations cycle" to account for the range of
possible outcomes of culture contacts between
diverse peoples. He attributed racial and cultural
contacts to the twin causes of migration and
conquest, and he posited that adjustments
subsequent to these contacts would involve the
processes of competition, conflict, accommodation,
and eventual assimilation (Park 1950:104).   In his
theoretical scheme, these processes were all
related to the problem of social control, with
special application to the need for instituting
political order in a community lacking a common
culture (Geschwender 1978:25).   Park called the
conditions of racial and cultural contact "racial
frontiers," and he located them within the
expansion of Europe and subsequent trade and
colonization (Park 1950:107-110).   Thus, he
situated his theory within the larger global
political and economic order, in contrast to those
who later built on his work. However, Park also
acknowledged that racial frontiers were created by
the large-scale immigration of those who were
racially and culturally distinct from the receiving
population.   In these contexts, a system of

subordination/ superordination was generally
instituted to regulate intergroup relations
(Geschwender 1978:22).

The contact of groups differing in customs and
behavior became translated into race relations only
when consciousness of differences moved to the
forefront (Park 1950:81). Consciousness of
differences brought about a sense of competition, a
pitting of one group against another. As a result,
conflict often erupted and had to be contained.
The most cost-effective way to contain conflict
was to install a system of institutionalized
political domination, that is, an hierarchical
social order, accepted tacitly by all ranks, in
which each group was assigned a clearly defined,
unambiguous position. Such systems constituted
accommodation (Geschwender 1978:21). Assimilation
was not the inevitable outcome of accommodation,
although the latter facilitated the process.
Rather, accommodation was an unstable system that
broke down at times. An example of such a
breakdown could be seen when unassimilated members
of subordinate groups refused to accept their lowly
positions and attempted to advance themselves
(Geschwender 1978:21). However, under conditions
of primary group contact, assimilation was
virtually unavoidable. It was only problematic
when social relations were of a secondary nature
(Park 1950:209-212).

The idea of assimilation arose out of the
context of immigration and was defined as "a
process of interpenetration and fusion in which
persons and groups acquire the memories,
sentiments, and attitudes of other persons or
groups, and, by sharing their experience and
history, are incorporated with them in a common
cultural life" (Park & Burgess 1924:735). To Park,
the process of assimilation, in essence, was a
cultural one of making people alike. It was the
acquisition of a new language, new attitudes, new
values and behavior. To Park's credit, he
envisioned the end product of this process as the
incorporation of small groups into a larger, more

inclusive one, and he recognized that this forging
of a corporate character was more problematic than
the fusion of cultures (Park 1950:207).   Indeed,
using the "Negro" as an example in his analysis of
the "race problem" in the United States, he
acknowledged that cultural likeness was
insufficient for incorporation, because the "Negro"
was culturally assimilated, but remained isolated
and segregated socially (Park 1950:212-215).   In
short, American society had succeeded in
"digesting" (assimilating) all human differences
except for the purely external one of skin color
(Park 1950:206).   However, Park was optimistic
that, in the long run, racial minorities would be
eliminated with the development of the modern state
(Geschwender 1978:23).   This was not to say that
exploitation would vanish, merely that racial
exploitation would be replaced by class
exploitation (Geschwender 1978:25).

In principle, Park's concept of assimilation
differed very little from the concept of
acculturation proposed by cultural anthropologists
(Herskovits 1958; Redfield, Linton & Herskovits
1936), and the two were often used
interchangeably.   In analytical usage and in
application, however, it seems to me that Park's
formulation is superior: he placed his ideas within
the scope of a larger world order and situated his
analysis within a general theory of social
interaction under conditions of asymmetrical power
relations.   Similarities and differences in the two
frameworks will be detailed below.

Scholars of the assimilation school and the
acculturation school were fascinated by culture
contact and its consequences.   Both schools
focussed attention on changes in patterns of
culture, in the transference of ideas, attitudes,
traditions, and customs from one human group to
another (Herskovits 1958).   Both acknowledged that
it was important to include in the analysis
situations of contact implying
dominance/subordination (Redfield et al. 1936).

Both schools conceptualized the process of acculturation as a linear, unidimensional one involving the extinguishing of one constellation of cultural traits and replacing them with a new repertoire with the passage of time. Neither school entertained the notion of biculturalism. Recent research suggests that the concept of biculturalism may more accurately account for the psycho-social adjustment of individuals and groups operating competently in more than one cultural context (Hannerz 1969:192; Szapocznik & Kurtines 1980). That is to say, acculturation may be a two-dimensional process involving accommodation to the host culture and retention of the original culture: in short, an additive process rather than one of replacement (Szapocznik & Kurtines 1980). In my opinion, writing as an immigrant equipped with more than one cultural repertoire to be activated when conducting myself in different cultural settings, the two-dimensional model better explains the cultural adaptation of immigrants and their first generation descendants. That is to say, I have acquired additional cultural repertoires without jettisoning previous ones.

The acculturation school diverged from the assimilation school in the former's obsession with the listing and cataloging of cultural traits, material and otherwise, and with determining their origins (provenience). Furthermore, the methods used by the acculturationists tended to depict relations between groups in terms of differences in trait inventories or the swapping of traits between "fixed isolates" over a fixed period of history (Herskovits 1958). In their analyses of acculturation, acculturationists betrayed an excessive preoccupation with the selection of traits, the reciprocal modification of traits in donor and recipient cultures, the traits offered by the donor group, traits selected by the receiving group, traits rejected by the latter, as well as the manner of integrating traits into the cultural patterns of the receiving group (Redfield et al. 1936).

In contrast, the assimilationists, as represented by Park, concerned themselves with the social processes brought about by culture contacts, particularly the relationship of these processes to systems of social control instituted to regulate social interaction and intergroup relations (Park & Burgess 1924:504-784). Most importantly, Park attached great significance to systems of institutionalized inequality in the maintenance of social order under conditions of racial and cultural pluralism. By diverting attention away from the elements of culture change and toward issues of race and unequal power relations and their role in retarding the formation of a corporate national character, Park and his contemporaries acknowledged a relationship between race contacts and the emergence of systems of domination which served to maintain economic advantage of one group over another.

THE REFINEMENT OF THE ASSIMILATION PARADIGM

Milton Gordon's (1964) work, Assimilation in American Life, has been considered a milestone in the study of race and ethnicity in the United States (Geschwender 1978). As a contribution in the assimilationist tradition, it revealed the nature of the assimilation process in American social life. By drawing a distinction between cultural behavior and social structure, Gordon (1964:67, 81) identified the key to American assimilation: it was to be found not in "cultural assimilation" or acculturation, as cultural anthropologists would have it, but in "structural assimilation" or social structural participation. Gordon (1964:77) perceived correctly that behavioral assimilation or acculturation was a necessary but not a sufficient condition for assimilation which he envisioned as a process encompassing many more dimensions. In other words, culture change was merely the first of many stages necessary to complete the process. It was possible, for example, for a social group to remain at this stage indefinitely without further forward movement, as illustrated by the case of black Americans (Gordon 1964:78).

Gordon conceptualized assimilation as a seven-stage process, the cornerstone of the entire edifice being the second phase, structural assimilation. Defined as the "large-scale entrance into cliques, clubs and institutions of the host society, on the primary group level" (Gordon 1964:71), structural assimilation was regarded as critical because it was a necessary condition from which all subsequent stages followed, and its absence constituted an obstacle to full societal incorporation. As primary group interaction, structural assimilation would pave the way toward marital assimilation or intermarriage between ethnic groups on a large scale, the third phase (Gordon 1964:80). Intermarriage, in turn, would promote the fourth phase, the "development of a sense of peoplehood based exclusively on the host society," or identificational assimilation (Gordon 1964:71). In this way, ethnic groups would lose their particularistic cultural identities, develop an "in-group" feeling, and become indistinguishable from members of the host society. Once these four stages occurred, the remaining ones would no longer be problematic. The fifth stage, attitude receptional assimilation or the absence of prejudice, and the sixth stage, behavior receptional assimilation or the absence of discrimination, would naturally ensue because there would be no distinct collectivities upon which to target prejudice and discrimination. Furthermore, the final and seventh stage, civic assimilation or the absence of ethnic power conflict, would also follow, once the interests of particularistic cultures disappeared (Gordon 1964:80).

Clearly, Gordon's notion of complete assimilation was utopian. He himself admitted that the American experience fell short of the model

(Gordon 1964:159). In fact, he viewed American society as a tapestry divided into parts based on race, religion, and -- minimally -- national origins, with social class divisions intersecting all three (Gordon 1964:160). Structural assimilation had only been achieved in the social worlds of intellectuals and artists, and even there, only to a limited extent. In short, the American condition was one of massive acculturation of all groups, coupled with "structural pluralism" or the maintenance of structurally separate subsocieties, those of Protestants, Catholics, Jews, and Blacks (Gordon 1964:159). While one may dispute whether or not acculturation of all groups obtains in America, it cannot be denied that structural pluralism exists. Structural pluralism has meant that social life has been carried out within structurally separate communities, each one composed of primary groups of families, cliques, associations, networks, organizations, and institutions (Gordon 1964:234). For example, blacks lived in a separate social world, with their own organizations and institutions, where they were isolated from meaningful primary group contacts with the white population (Gordon 1964:163).

However, on a day-to-day basis, the functioning units of society were actually smaller sub-units which Gordon called "ethclasses" (1964:160). These may be defined as "subcommunities based on the intersection of ethnic group and social class factors" (Gordon 1964:161), or networks of people who interact with each other because of similarity in ethnicity and social status. The importance of ethclass lay in the fact that intimate, primary relationships tended to be confined to the ethclass. Conversely, interaction outside the ethclass unit tended toward impersonal, secondary group contact (Gordon 1964:234). Moreover, like units of ethclass were often connected with one another across geographical boundaries by friendships, organizations, and institutions (Gordon 1964:161). That ethclass was a guiding principle of social interaction could be seen in

the case of blacks.   Although they lived in a
world apart, blacks were also differentiated along
class lines.   These social class cleavages evolved
from patterns of differential social interaction
with whites, dating back to the days of slavery.
The result was variation in the degree of
acculturation among the black population, with
greater acculturation being associated with higher
social status.   In this way, the black upper class
came to resemble the white Protestant upper-middle
class in terms of values, attitudes, and behavior
(Gordon 1964:166-173).   They nevertheless lived in
a separate social universe.

There is no question that Gordon's (1964)
insights into the structural impediments to
assimilation have been valuable.   He discerned
correctly that the process of immigrant adjustment
was not simply a matter of acculturation.   Rather,
the crux of the problem lay in the incorporation of
immigrants into the institutional spheres of
society.   Others before him had reasoned similarly,
most notably, S.N. Eisenstadt (1954) in The
Absorption of Immigrants.   Eisenstadt interpreted
the problem of the successful adaptation of
immigrants as a question of the immigrants'
capacity to perform successfully basic roles
inherent in the main institutional spheres of the
social structure of the absorbing country
(Eisenstadt 1954:6-14).   Thus, it was not so much
that Gordon's (1964) ideas differed radically from
those of Eisenstadt, whose analyses conformed to
the structural-functional tradition, but rather
that Gordon elaborated on them and, at the same
time, linked the phenomenon of race with the
phenomenon of class by constructing the concept of
"ethclass."   It may be said, however, that his
treatment of both issues left a great deal to be
desired.

Gordon (1964) clearly acknowledged a
relationship between race/ethnicity and the system
of stratification.   What Gordon (1964) failed to
apprehend was the raison d'etre of such a system.
He merely accepted the existence of the system of

inequality as a given, without admitting to the useful functions it served in the effective exploitation of immigrants and racial minorities by dominant/host groups. With respect to the immigrants, Gordon (1964) did not identify their mode of structural incorporation into the peripheral sectors of the economy during the early phases of their resettlement (cf. Portes 1981, for an illuminating analysis of the differential modes of immigrant adjustment as a function of their structural incorporation into different sectors of the economy). Nor did Gordon (1964) chart the course of their ascent from the secondary labor market upward into the primary labor market at an auspicious moment of expansion in United States economic history (Geschwender 1978). Otherwise put, Gordon (1964) did not specify how it came to be that some immigrants and racial minorities rose to occupy positions of high and middle status, while others did not achieve upward mobility and remained at the bottom. Or, simply put, how did "ethclass" come about?

The question of racial assimilation is another domain in which Gordon's analysis may be found wanting. Despite his recognition of the structural impediments to assimilation, Gordon (1964) placed excessive emphasis on the role of prejudice in non-assimilation. But the psychodynamics of prejudice operate on the level of individuals, or categories of individuals, not on the level of institutions. Hence, prejudice on the part of individuals cannot explain institutional barriers to racial integration. Nevertheless, Gordon (1964) believed that prejudice would fade away in due course, and once prejudice was eradicated, all forms of discrimination and racial problems would cease to exist. In short, Gordon (1964) found nothing essentially wrong with the direction in which American society was headed and certainly did not believe that American political and economic institutions were in need of reform. Indeed, with specific reference to the question of black structural separation, Gordon (1964:245-251) adamantly opposed governmental intervention to institute racial desegregation in public arenas and explicitly advocated public policies to that effect.

In many respects Gordon's philosophy was consistent with others of the assimilationist school who believed that assimilation was both inevitable and in keeping with the ideals of democracy. While Gordon himself did not regard assimilation as inescapable, he did equate it with the process of individual upward mobility made possible by equality of opportunity. Some of his colleagues (Glazer & Moynihan 1963) applied similar logic, in the tradition of American Liberalism, to account for the status of blacks in American society. They argued from the vantage point of the "Blacks as Immigrants" analogy which posited a commonality between the historical experiences of European immigrants and the contemporary circumstances faced by blacks. By thus reducing the problem of race to one of low socio-economic status, which they considered remediable by ambition and achievement, they reasoned that blacks would repeat the mobility patterns of European immigrants earlier in this century. When blacks as a group failed to do so, they explained it as a lack of achievement motivation (Glazer & Moynihan 1963). In addition, they expected racism to disappear because it was incompatible with the requirements of modern social organization in industrialized and urbanized societies. Therefore, they did not even entertain the notion that racism and racial cleavages were an integral part of America. Unlike Park (1950) and the early assimilationists, later assimilationists refused to concede a relationship between race and the emergence of systems of domination.

THE NEW IMMIGRATION: TERRA NOVA AND CHALLENGE

Despite claims that the assimilation paradigm
has become passe in academic circles, there is
evidence that this theoretical framework continues
to guide much contemporary research on immigration
and ethnic and race relations. For instance,
Massey (1981), in a review article on the
assimilation of New Immigrants into American
society, noted that there was concern on the part
of policy-makers, as well as the general public,
over the capacity of the United States to absorb
millions of foreigners. He analyzed the New
Immigration along six dimensions, familism,
fertility, residential segregation, political
participation, intermarriage, and social mobility.
He concluded that overall, the New Immigrants
appeared to be well on their way towards
assimilation, with two exceptions: Mexicans and
Puerto Ricans (Massey 1981:77-79). Of the two
groups, Puerto Ricans were the least socially
integrated in terms of residential segregation,
restriction with respect to intermarriage, and
confinement to the secondary labor market (Massey
1981:78). Puerto Ricans also resembled black
Americans in these respects (Massey 1981:78). It
might be said that black Caribbean immigrants fit
this description as well.

In a more recent review, Hirschman (1983)
re-assessed the melting pot myth along the
dimensions of social mobility, segregation,
intermarriage, and attitudes, with reference to
both immigrants and American minorities. His
conclusions are germane to the problem of black
immigrants in this country. More specifically, he
noted that the scaffolding of socio-economic
stratification and institutional segregation
continues to rest on the foundation of race for
blacks and Puerto Ricans. Along the dimension of
social mobility, for example, the socio-economic
chasm between blacks and whites has persisted,
although this has not been the trend for Asians

and Hispanics (Hirschman 1983:416). Residential segregation between blacks and whites has remained at high levels with only slight variation according to social class (Hirschman 1983:416). Closely linked with residential segregation, segregation in education has declined in recent years, but the prospects of this trend continuing are not high (Hirschman 1983:416). Based on these findings, it was inferred that, in the final analysis, the obstacles confronting blacks in America are of a different order than those facing other ethnic minorities (Hirschman 1983:417).

In light of these circumstances, advocates of ethnic pluralism have suggested that the goal of assimilation should be dismissed as anachronistic (Dominguez 1975). Instead, scholars and policy-makers alike should look towards ethnic pluralism as the new organizing principle of American society. If ethnic pluralism is taken to mean cultural pluralism, it should not be problematic because a certain degree of cultural diversity has always existed and been tolerated in America. Some have even considered it desirable because it has added color to an otherwise monochromatic cultural landscape. However, if ethnic pluralism means structural pluralism, then it must be remembered that pluralism's motto is not "separate, but equal". Rather, it is "separate and unequal." It is worth recalling that structural pluralism hinges on inequality between dominant groups and racial minorities. Therefore, the question becomes how to achieve equality while being forced to remain structurally separate (Steinberg 1981). For, as Van den Berghe (1981:224) insightfully pointed out, the problem of assimilation is not so much one of willingness to be assimilated on the part of immigrants, as it is one of acceptance by the dominant group.

With specific reference to the assimilation of immigrants of color, the only strategy worth pursuing would appear to be that of "ethnic groups as interest groups." Indeed, as long as fifteen years ago, Metzger (1971:638) suggested that

accepting the theorem that racism is central to
American culture and society also requires
accepting the corollary that racism could only be
eroded by prolonged social conflict and
re-organization of institutional structures. This
is because racism is a key ingredient in
buttressing present socio-economic arrangements
(Metzger 1971:637). The dilemma of racial
inequality in America can best be addressed, in my
opinion, by the incorporation of New Immigrants of
color into the racial minorities of this country
because the problems confronting such New
Immigrants are not unlike those that have been
encountered by racial minorities for several
centuries, the most formidable of these being
institutional racism.

It is of critical importance to distinguish
race prejudice from racism that is
institutionalized (Blauner 1972:8-10). Racial
hatred and stereotyped attitudes towards racial
groups are necessary but not sufficient conditions
for institutionalization. They are attributes of
individuals or groups that lack systematization.
Institutional racism, on the other hand,
systematically attempts to limit full participation
by subordinate racial groups in essential areas of
social, economic, and political life by building
restrictions into the operation of bureaucratic
structures (Blauner 1972:10). One result has been
erosion of the dignity and self-respect of
non-white peoples. To prevent such an experience,
it would behoove non-white immigrants to join ranks
with their native-born counterparts to challenge
patterns of racial control and to undermine the
racial order. The conservative "backlash" which
has occurred in reaction to the Civil Rights
Movement and other social upheavals that took place
in America in the 1960's and early 1970's is
gaining strength and momentum. In response, it
will be necessary to enlist the forces of the New
Immigrants to mount a new offensive movement aimed
at racial equality. To the extent that the
population growth of the United States derives from

immigration, the immigration of people of color in
vast numbers will surely have a profound impact on
the social landscape of America.

It was with this concern in mind that
Bryce-Laporte (1980:459-472) declared the New
Immigration to be a challenge to "the sociological
imagination." Observing that the Immigration and
Nationality Act of 1965 had essentially gone
unnoticed by social scientists, despite the fact
that it revolutionized a century of racist,
exclusionist, and discriminatory positions on
immigration by the United States, he lamented the
"abdication of the study of immigration" by
American scholars (Bryce-Laporte 1980:462). The
fact that these sweeping changes in the ethnic and
racial composition of the United States population
were ignored and went undocumented by social
scientists during an era in which other radical
transformations of American society were taking
place, made it even more reprehensible.

This void in scholarship has fuelled the
current movement to restrict immigration. Some
social scientists number among those
anti-immigration advocates who operate out of
historical short-sightedness and who misuse social
science in the process (Bryce-Laporte 1980:465).
Their tunnel vision permits them to see no further
than the confines of national boundaries, so they
perceive the New Immigration as solely a domestic,
that is, American, political problem, relevant only
to this moment in time. They fail to see
connections linking the United States with other
nations, as well as the active part played by the
United States in stimulating global population
movements (Bryce-Laporte 1980:465). Acting on
limited knowledge, they are determined to preserve
present inequalities at home and abroad. They are
oblivious to the Janus-faced history of American
immigration which extends, on the one hand, an open
door to immigrants, and on the other hand, confines
them to marginal, peripheral sectors of society
because of their polluting power (Bryce-Laporte
1980:465).

Fear of immigrants of color also fuels anti-immigrant hysteria. A general alarm has been raised by a distorted sense of the threats posed by these immigrants and a plethora of social ills wrongly attributed to them (Bryce-Laporte 1980:464). Supporters of anti-immigration sentiments are recapitulating history by resurrecting the "yellow peril" and creating afresh the "brown peril" and "black peril." However, a just and equitable solution to the problems of immigration and inequality cannot be constructed out of panic. Meticulous and well-informed social analysis is still indispensable to the formulation of effective policies and the undertaking of successful legislative action.

Inspired by C. Wright Mills' (1959:7) appeal to social scientists to accept responsibility for their roles in the making of history by means of "the sociological imagination," Bryce-Laporte (1980:469) proposed a similar challenge for latter-day social scientists to recast the issues surrounding the New Immigration into "classical analysis of the interconnections of biography, history and society/world." The gauntlet being thrown down before contemporary American scholarship is to capture the complexity of the New Immigration, to fathom how the newcomers will alter the shape and substance of a nation that was born of immigration and received form and content from it (Bryce-Laporte 1980:468), and to grasp the making of world history by examining United States relations with those countries sending immigrants (Bryce-Laporte 1980:470). Various levels of phenomena will merit investigation, among them, global political-economic structures, transnational linkages, international stratification, as well as processes accompanying immigration, such as ethnification. The treatment received by immigrants from important institutions of American society will also need to be addressed, as will the cultural, psychological, and socio-economic characteristics of the immigrants and the changes they experience (Bryce-Laporte 1980:463).

CHAPTER II

THE CARIBBEAN EXODUS IN HISTORICAL CONTEXT

THE CARIBBEAN EXODUS

Ever since European settlement in the region, emigration has been, and continues to be, a quintessential feature of West Indian societies (Bryce-Laporte 1976; Lowenthal 1972). Indeed, Marshall (1982) estimates that the Caribbean exodus from the Commonwealth Caribbean has been going on for 150 years. Although there has been movement of people internal to the region, from small to larger islands, the main thrust of population movement has been outwards, following the path of employment opportunities. For instance, between 1850 and World War I, West Indian migration to Central America was stimulated by wage work available in the building of the Panama Canal and also in the banana plantations of Costa Rica (Foner 1978; Palmer 1974).

Since World War I, emigration out of the Commonwealth Caribbean has been toward two major destinations: North America (both the United States and Canada) and the United Kingdom (Marshall 1982). This is partly a function of economic history and partly a function of immigration policy in the receiving countries. The massive exodus of West Indians towards the metropoles has been attributed by "push-pull" theorists to the underdeveloped character of Caribbean economies.

Dependence, economic and otherwise, is the hallmark
of this condition.

As a legacy of colonialism, it is perpetuated
today by neo-colonial governments in collaboration
with multinational corporations in a slightly
altered guise (Foner 1978; Watson 1976). This
dependence is manifested economically in the form
of chronic structural unemployment and
underemployment. Extremely limited job
opportunities and a high population growth rate
make it imperative for many to leave (Lowenthal
1972). The magnet drawing West Indians to their
destinations in North America and the United
Kingdom is the substantial wage differential
between their homelands, in which it is low, and
their destinations, in which it is high, as well as
the availability of jobs (Palmer 1974).

IMMIGRATION POLICIES IN RECEIVING COUNTRIES

Immigration policies in the metropoles of
Europe and North America have played a role in
shaping the course of Caribbean migration. In
historical perspective, the policies in these
receiving countries may be characterized as
ambivalent, at best, since they fluctuate between
the extremes of severe restrictions and free
movement (Keely & Elwell 1981:182). Three
historical landmarks punctuate the history of
immigration to the United States (Marshall
1982:6). The first of these was the Chinese
Exclusion Act passed in 1882, by nomenclature
designed to keep out the Chinese who were perceived
to be a menace. Prior to this, admission to the
United States had been relatively unimpeded.
However, the influx of large numbers of Chinese in
California during the goldrush, and the racial
unrest that followed, prompted legislation intended
to curtail entry of certain racial groups in order

to preserve the racial composition of the U.S. population.

The second landmark was the National Origins Act passed in 1924 which was a continuing expression of the previously mentioned racial bias. This time it was aimed at excluding the Japanese, as well as other non-white immigrants. The 1924 act brought West Indian immigration to a virtual halt. However, due to a labor shortage during World War II, the flow of West Indians resumed at that time but was again curtailed in 1952 by the passage of the McCarren-Walter Act. This law established a quota system limiting each country to a very small number of entrants; Western European countries were excepted (Palmer 1974).

Consequently, emigration from the Commonwealth Caribbean was deflected to the United Kingdom which, at that time, virtually held open doors to settlement by colonial British subjects because their labor was badly needed in the post-World War II boom. By the 1960's however, colonial immigration from the West Indies, India and Pakistan had accelerated at such a pace that Britain became alarmed and introduced the Commonwealth Immigrants Act in 1962, effectively blocking further entry except for dependents of those colonials already in the United Kingdom (Foner 1978). Once more, West Indian migration was redirected to the United States, increasing by seven-fold between 1962 and 1972 (Palmer 1974).

This was made possible by the third landmark in U.S. immigration legislation in 1965, which liberalized policies dramatically. The Immigration Act of 1965 introduced several innovations that have had a dramatic effect on the character and pattern of immigration to the U.S. First of all, it eliminated the national origins quota system which had severely limited entry except from Western Europe and replaced it with hemispheric ceilings, establishing parity among independent nations in each hemisphere (Bryce-Laporte 1976; Keely & Elwell 1981). It accomplished this in phases over a period of three

years, taking full effect in 1968. Another
departure was the introduction of a labor
certification requirement, for admissions based on
occupational criteria, making it necessary for the
Department of Labor to certify that a U.S. citizen
was not being displaced from the job market by the
immigrant (Keely & Elwell 1981). This requirement
had the effect of redistributing the occupational
characteristics of the immigrant population. The
number of professional workers rose sharply. The
number of blue collar technical and skilled workers
also increased somewhat, but the number of
clerical, sales and farm workers declined
significantly. Those admitted on occupational
grounds, therefore, were better educated and
trained.

However, this skewed distribution was balanced
by a countervailing force in that family
reunification criteria were given priority over
occupational preferences, allowing spouses,
children and parents of those already citizens of
the U.S. to be sponsored free of labor
certification considerations. Further, the
admission of family members was to take place
outside of hemispheric ceiling allowances (Keely &
Elwell 1981).

To reiterate, the 1965 legislation has had a
profound effect on immigration in the United
States. In volume alone, admissions have reached
unprecedented levels. The annual average level of
entries rose from 290,062 between 1961 and 1965 to
a high of 600,000 for the year 1978 alone (Keely &
Elwell 1981:188). The complexion of immigration
has changed. As Table 1 shows, European
immigration has declined in both absolute and
relative terms, while Asian immigration has soared.
Immigration from Africa and Oceania has increased
considerably. Immigration from the Caribbean and
Central America falls under the category of North
America in Table 1. It can be seen that while it
has increased in absolute numbers, in relative
terms, the percentage has declined. Immigration

from South America has declined in relative and absolute terms (Keely & Elwell 1981).

The year 1986 has proved to be another milestone in the history of U.S. immigration. The liberal philosophy embodied in the 1965 Immigration Act resulted in radical transformations in the racial composition of the American population. At the same time, there has been an influx of undocumented workers, mostly of Hispanic origin. Their conspicuously large numbers in California and elsewhere has generated fear that undocumented laborers are displacing U.S. citizens from the job market. Analysts focussing on the contemporary re-structuring of the U.S. labor market contend that this fear is unfounded (Sassen-Koob 1981). Notwithstanding, enough alarm has been generated among American workers to create demands for immigration reform. In response, yet another Immigration and Control Act became law in 1986.

The declared objective of the Simpson-Rodino Bill (1986) was to bring illegal immigration to a halt. The method of restriction to be used was employer sanctions, i.e., penalties to be imposed on employers who knowingly hire undocumented workers. Only its most ardent supporters believe that this piece of legislation will be even moderately successful in stemming the tide of immigrant labor. As one leading scholar of undocumented Mexican immigration has pointed out, over the past thirteen years, employer sanctions have been tested in more than twenty other nations, and ten states in the U.S., with resounding failure (Cornelius 1984).

Without exception, penalties aimed at employers in other countries have failed to diminish the hiring of illegal immigrants. Instead, the penalties have been borne by the workers themselves, being made more vulnerable than ever to exploitation. Employers have taken advantage of the threats of sanctions to justify imposing lower wages, more hazardous working conditions on the immigrant workers and eliminating fringe benefits. As Cornelius (1984) put it: "this is a prescription for further degradation of wages and labor standards in the United States."

More to the point, Cornelius (1984) discovered in his research that only 6 percent of his sample of California firms would try to replace illegal workers with legal ones or with U.S. Citizens. In addition, his research suggested that only large, highly-capitalized, high-waged businesses would alter their hiring practices. This is largely due to the fact that these larger companies have options open to them which small, low-waged, non-union firms do not. Among these alternatives is exporting their capital and production to "cheap-labor" countries.

It is precisely this latter alternative that points to the critical flaw in Simpson-Rodino reasoning: it is pure folly to attempt to curb the flow of immigrant labor into the U.S. labor market, without understanding the economic forces that propel multitudes from the Third World to the United States. Attempting to limit the inflow without simultaneously prohibiting the flight of U.S. capital overseas to places where labor is less expensive is even more futile. The two phenomena are simply two sides of the same coin. To deal with one and ignore the other is plainly absurd.

It should not be inferred from the foregoing that the United States has no right to restrict immigration in order to protect the rights of its citizens. Indeed, it is a nation's duty to do so. What is at issue here, is the method being proposed to accomplish this goal, one that has been demonstrated to be ineffectual. Critics of the Simpson-Rodino statute charge that besides failing to deter the entry of new migrants from Mexico and Central America, an unintended consequence of this bill is to promote and condone underemployment and discriminatory hiring practices, targetted at those with "foreign" physical attributes, mainly Latinos and Asians, justified by threats of penalties. Ironically, black immigrants will most likely escape this particular form of discrimination as a function of their invisibility.

Notwithstanding these changes in immigration legislation, there is yet to emerge any well-defined, coherent political philosophy or policy on international migration. U.S. immigration legislation, the Simpson-Rodino Bill being its most recent expression, has proceeded on the basis of reflexive action to global economic trends while simultaneously treating international migration as a purely domestic problem, without linkages to the international economy. Such a position is clearly foolish. Estimates of the Caribbean presence in the U.S., including all language groups, both documented and undocumented, is approximately four million (Dominguez & Dominguez 1981). This immigrant stream stems from the economic and social problems of the region. As such, it demands more serious attention than that which has been the hallmark of U.S. concern in the region to date: simple posturing aimed at containment of its rival superpower. At the very least, the New Immigration poses a dilemma, even if perceived as strictly a domestic problem.

Policy trends in Canada have essentially paralleled those described for the United States. It should be noted, however, that the "great expansion," the Canadian analogue of the New Immigration, took place between 1962 and 1967. In 1967, new immigrant regulations were adopted that emphasized manpower needs for Canadian economic development as well as the goal of family reunion, based on a point system (Keely & Elwell 1981:199). Between 1967 and 1971 Canadian immigration declined but increased again after 1971, enough to warrant a national inquiry on immigration and population, resulting in the Immigration Act of 1976. Of primary concern were the issues of volume, ethnic composition and urban concentration of the immigrants. The ethnic issue was stimulated by the increase in Asian and West Indian immigration. A new point system was developed stressing manpower needs even more than previously, mainly because the rise in immigration had occurred during an economic recession. Canadian policy, therefore, also lacks

a well-defined position and proceeds on the basis
of short term gains (Keely & Elwell 1981:200-205).

POLITICAL ECONOMY OF THE SENDING SOCIETIES

    Mintz (1971) has convincingly argued that the
raison d'etre of Caribbean societies over the past
four centuries has been solely to satisfy the needs
of Europe. As a system of overseas agricultural
capitalism, the plantation system established by
Europe in the New World in the eighteenth century,
was founded on monocrop cultivation. In the case
of the Caribbean, sugar was produced as a commodity
for export to overseas markets. The Plantation,
then, was a mode of production that bore the
closest resemblance to rural factories engaged in
industrial production, before the arrival of the
Industrial Revolution (Mintz 1971). As such, it
has linked Caribbean economies irrevocably with the
fortunes of Europe, and more recently, with those
of North America.
    Dependency has been the leitmotif of the
Caribbean economic order ever since the days of
European colonialism. With the advent of political
independence in the last two decades, political
domination by the colonial power has come to a
halt. Nevertheless, in the realm of economics, a
dependent system persists as Caribbean economies
continue to be subordinate appendages of
metropolitan capital and enterprise, articulated
with the global economic order through metropolitan
centers which function as loci of control over the
expansion of trade and market relations,
deflecting profits and surplus away from
re-investment in the Caribbean, to the source of
capital, now North America instead of Europe
(Beckford 1972). Although in some Caribbean
territories the substance has changed, remnants of
Plantation structure endure in the form of foreign
ownership of production, an orientation toward

export production for external markets, inadequate production for local consumption, and its corollary, the necessity to import basic foodstuffs and manufactured goods (Beckford 1972).

Since political independence, many Caribbean governments have made noble efforts to break the vise of export agriculture based on "King Sugar," by diversifying into food production for local use and by building up a viable industrial sector (Cross 1979:32). This is all the more expedient because agriculture is more labor-intensive than any other industry. However, Plantation dependence is difficult to vanquish. The lion's share of farm land as well as the best quality farm land is concentrated in the hands of foreign-based corporations.

For instance, in Trinidad, the sugar industry was dominated by Caroni Ltd., a subsidiary of Tate and Lyle, a huge multinational sugar-producing corporation based in London. Plantations, by monopolizing the most and the best land, leave little land for small proprietors. This guarantees that the rural populations would be forced to seek wage labor on the Plantation and become a rural proletariat. The Plantation has also introduced mechanization to improve efficiency. The outcome of these developments has been increasing rural unemployment, compelling many to migrate to the cities and some to migrate overseas (Cross 1979).

The rural population is moving to the urban periphery to seek wage work because the rural sectors are unable to provide sufficient employment. Industries other than agriculture furnish some jobs but not enough to keep the labor force fully employed. It is estimated, for instance, that the bauxite industry for the entire Caribbean employs no more than 20,000 individuals (Cross 1979). Mineral and petroleum export industries have proliferated in the larger territories but are capital-intensive and require importing capital from abroad and securing markets (Girvan 1975). Rather than solving the problem of unemployment, capital-intensive industries generate further problems because they create a labor aristocracy that is paid high wages, and as a result, standards for high levels of consumption are established.

In addition, high wages in mining and petroleum industries cause wages in the manufacturing and service sectors to rise. Manufacturing costs also rise and make local products non-competitive with imports. This, in turn, promotes mechanization and negatively affects employment (Levitt & Best 1975). Manufacturing is also a mixed blessing because Caribbean societies have not accumulated sufficient capital to invest in manufacture and therefore depend on external sources to provide capital while they supply the local labor (Levitt & Best 1975). Tourism has not lived up to the expectations of most Caribbean countries. The industry is vulnerable to global recessions and at best provides seasonal employment. Often capital investment from overseas hotel chains becomes necessary in order to import the kinds of luxury goods and services demanded by the tastes of affluent tourists (Cross 1979:42).

The conclusion is inescapable that unemployment is the central economic and social problem of the Caribbean. It is ironic that Caribbean societies have been transformed from economies with an insatiable appetite for labor to those with a substantial labor surplus. There is widespread unemployment of colossal proportions which range from 15 percent to 25 percent of the labor force. It has been asserted that the Caribbean suffers from "structural unemployment," generated by the importing of capital-intensive technology designed by and for economies in which labor costs are high. These technologies are inappropriate for economies with a labor surplus and a shortage of capital (Levitt & Best 1975). To aggravate the situation, close contact with metropolitan countries stimulates the emulation of metropolitan consumption patterns and requires the importing of luxury goods. These consumption patterns are exacerbated with the rise of comparative affluence

resulting from the growth of the middle class and
the birth of a labor aristocracy. Advertising and
the mass media make the problem even worse
(Patterson 1978). All of these factors exert
strong pressures for population movement both
overseas and internally from rural areas to the
urban periphery, the latter culminating in "urban
sprawl" (Patterson 1978). A two-stage process
appears to be operating: movement from the country
to the city: then, when employment is not
forthcoming, movement overseas with high hopes of
better opportunities there (Cross 1979:71).

SOCIAL STRUCTURE OF THE SENDING SOCIETIES

From a demographic perspective, Caribbean
societies are historically unique in that their
indigenous populations were totally decimated,
necessitating the importation and transplantation
to the region of coerced multitudes from the
African continent and, later, Asia in an
astonishing demographic experiment. As a type of
colonial exploitation of human resources,
Plantation Slavery was unparalleled in pervading
all aspects of life as a "total institution."
Indeed, slavery left its indelible stamp on
Caribbean social structure by providing the
blueprint for social relations. Caribbean
societies are divided along lines of social class
which correspond to race and gradations in skin
color (Lowenthal 1972:81).
    In colonial times, this color-class hierarchy
was a social pyramid at the top of which was a
small upper class composed of white or
light-skinned individuals who were either local
landed-gentry or administrators. Power was in
their hands. In the middle were people who were
intermediate both in skin color and social status,
the result of widespread "miscegenation" between
white masters and slave women. As a buffer between

the plantocracy and the folk at the bottom, the
middle classes relentlessly pursued social
advancement.   They were obsessed with physical
markers of social status, particularly gradations
in skin color.   It was possible to circumvent the
ascriptive system based on race via two avenues of
upward social mobility.   One was education and
occupational advancement.   Until recently this was
only an option for men, as the status of a family
hinged on the occupation of the male head.   The
other was marriage to lighter-skinned persons
(Braithwaite 1975).

Because both the middle and the lower classes
were non-white, the social class boundaries between
them tended to be vague if only the criterion of
race was considered.   Distinct differences in
social institutions served to reinforce these
boundaries (M.G. Smith 1965).   One institution that
revealed sharp divergences in the culture and
behavior of the elite, the middle class and the
peasantry or urban proletariat, was religion.   The
lower class preferred evangelical and revivalist
forms of Christianity and religions with clear
retention of Africanisms, while the middle class
took European religion very seriously, adhering
devoutly to denominations like the Methodists and
the Presbyterians.   Although not very devout, the
elite clung to the bastions of social prestige such
as Anglicanism or Roman Catholicism (Braithwaite
1975; Lowenthal 1972).   Another institutional
disparity was in the domain of the law.   Lower
class individuals were commonly subject to police
harassment, to differential prosecution for
gambling, to harsh punishment for moderate crimes
and to unfair legal penalties (Braithwaite 1975).

The socio-cultural gulf separating the middle
from the lower classes was most apparent in the
institution of the family.   Mating customs among
the rural and urban folk tended to follow a
sequential pattern, beginning with "visiting"
unions between two persons living in separate
households.   This was followed by "faithful
concubinage" or common-law-marriage in which the

partners shared a household that often included
children from former liaisons. The final stage of
formal marriage was characteristically deferred
until later life because being mature and able to
support a wife was regarded as necessary (Lowenthal
1972). For this reason, members of the lower class
often had children by different partners before
formal marriage took place, but they were not
stigmatized by illegitimacy, as defined by
Euro-American culture. Although the elite and the
middle class of the Caribbean married early and had
stable conjugal unions, they did not regard lower
class conduct as pathological, as it is regarded in
the United States, but accepted it as a genuine
distinction between the classes (Lowenthal
1972:113). Also, in contradistinction to
Euro-American norms, a system of bilateral extended
kin ties cross-cut all three social classes in the
Caribbean. These widespread links were enduring
and encompassed relatives who were not only
genealogically but also geographically distant
(Lowenthal 1972:105).

Attention should be drawn, however, to the fact
that the color-class hierarchy delineated above
embraces only what is known as "creole" society.
The term "creole" refers to persons and things
locally-born in the West Indies, of European or
African origin, or mixtures thereof (Lowenthal
1972:32-33). Therefore, "creole" culture is an
unique, local culture synthesizing elements from
both Europe and Africa to form a blend that is
distinct from the cultures of either homeland
(Patterson 1975:316-319). Instrumental aspects of
"creole" culture such as politics, economics,
education and law derive chiefly from European
institutions, whereas the expressive components
such as art, music dance, literature and drama are
founded on African traditions (Patterson
1975:316-319). It follows that "creolization" is
the process of acquiring "creole" culture, an
amalgam shaped in the New World.

To persist in the practice of Old World
culture, be it from Europe, Africa or Asia, is to

remain aloof and apart from local social life, and to remain outside the system of social rewards. Thus, there is much pressure to become "creolized" (Ryan 1972:24). In most West Indian societies, the "creole" segment comprises the greater part of the population. For instance, of the three largest territories in the Anglophone Caribbean, Jamaica, Guyana and Trinidad, the racial and ethnic makeup of Jamaica is typical of most of the Caribbean in the sense that its population is 90 percent black, 5 percent mixed, less than 2 percent white, 2 percent East Indian and only 1 percent Chinese. In other words, only a tiny fraction of the people are not "creole" in that they are either East Indian or Chinese in culture.

Trinidad and Guyana are anomalous in that the populations there are divided almost equally between those of African descent and those of East Indian descent. In the case of Guyana, East Indians comprise 50% of the population (twenty-five times that of Jamaica,) while those of African descent comprise only about one-third of the population, (one-third that of Jamaica). The mixed-race segment (mulatto) is also twice that of Jamaica. Guyana is also unique in having an Amerindian segment that makes up 4 percent of its population; Amerindians are virtually extinct elsewhere in the Caribbean.

In Trinidad the population distribution is more like that of Guyana than that of Jamaica but the proportion of black to East Indian is reversed. Whereas in Guyana blacks comprised one-third of the population, in Trinidad they make up almost one-half. And, whereas in Guyana East Indians made up one-half of the population, in Trinidad they comprise over one-third. Also, the mixed-race segment in Trinidad is larger than those of either Guyana or Jamaica (three times that of Jamaica). Furthermore, in all three territories, the Chinese segment makes up about 1 percent or slightly less.

The point of this discussion is that the East Indian and the Chinese segments, in many respects, exist outside of the "creole" color-class hierarchy. And, as previously mentioned, those who find themselves outside of the "creole" color-class hierarchy also find themselves excluded from social status, political power and to a lesser extent, wealth (Lowenthal 1972:145). In terms of social position, both the East Indians and the Chinese began life in Trinidad as indentured laborers at the bottom of the social pyramid (Lowenthal 1972:145, 202). Following the abolition of slavery in 1838, both groups from Asia were imported to replace the labor force on the sugar plantations lost through emancipation. They therefore occupied very lowly class positions alongside lower class blacks (Ryan 1972:20). The major difference was that the East Indians were very different culturally from those of African descent, even though both groups lived in abject poverty. East Indians clung to their cultural institutions which were not destroyed as were those of the Africans during slavery. Eighty percent of them continued to observe their Hindu traditions and the other 20 percent their Muslim customs (Ryan 1972:21).

Relations between East Indians and blacks in Trinidad have never been amicable, although the hostility between them has never escalated to the point of bloodshed, as was the case in Guyana before independence. The conflict is of a multi-dimensional nature: cultural, economic and political. Blacks looked down upon East Indians because they were culturally strange and socially isolated. They also perceived them as an economic threat to their recent emancipation. For their part, East Indians regarded blacks as savage and feared pollution from them (Ryan 1972:21). These stereotypes persisted as long as the East Indians remained an agricultural people on the Plantations, and the majority of them did so. A small minority, however, moved to the city, became urbanized, entered the retail trade and became "creolized" (Ryan 1972:21). In other words, upward mobility is partly a function of becoming creolized, of being

incorporated into the creole hierarchy. In the
second half of this century, greater and greater
numbers of East Indians have become creolized.

What about the Chinese? They preceded the East
Indians as indentured laborers on the sugar
plantations. During this time they also occupied a
lowly position in the system of stratification.
When their contracts expired, they quickly fled
agriculture and entered the retail trade. They
rapidly became urbanized and, more importantly,
"creolized" (Lowenthal 1972:202-208). In contrast
to the East Indians who were mostly endogamous, the
Chinese freely mated with black women (Ryan
1972:23-24). This was partly the result of the
shortage of Chinese women in Trinidad, since women
were by custom left behind in China. As a result,
a large part of the population in Trinidad labelled
as "Chinese," actually share both African and
Chinese ancestry and are not "racially pure." More
significantly, however, they are not very Chinese
in a cultural sense. Most do not speak any dialect
of the Chinese language and the majority have no
knowledge of Chinese history or tradition with the
possible exception of food. Even those who are
"racially pure" are not "culturally pure." Their
economic success has been at least partially
determined by their "creolization"; their ascent
into the middle class has also been made possible
by their light skin color (Ryan 1972:24). Both of
these combined have placed them in the position of
forming a buffer between the East Indians and the
blacks in their conflicts (Ryan 1972:24).

This is not to say that the color-class
hierarchy, to the extent that it exists today, in
itself provides the motive force behind emigration.
Rather, it is being suggested that it is the
educational system, patterned after the European
model, buttressing disparities in social class,
that effectively inhibits social advancement for
the majority of West Indians today. As some
Caribbean scholars have put it: "Educational
opportunities and life chances were rigidly
circumscribed by the social structure, which also

conditioned the development of educational institutions" (Rubin & Zavalloni 1969:181).

The lure of possibilities in mobility comes chiefly from abroad. While it is believed by all that education is the sine qua non of upward mobility and that handicaps of ancestry and race may be transcended by acquiring an education, in the West Indies education is a resource to which there is unequal access (Lowenthal 1972; Rubin & Zavalloni 1969). It is precisely because personal achievement is so drastically constrained that it becomes necessary for the socially ambitious to emigrate to improve their education and skills, and hopefully, to acquire wealth.

During colonial times, the structure of the educational system in the former British West Indies was based on a classical British philosophy of education intended to benefit only the elite (Lowenthal 1972; Rubin & Zavalloni 1969). There was, and still is, an hierarchical ranking of schools in terms of prestige as well as educational standards, at both the primary and secondary school levels. Schools range in quality from excellent to abysmal. Predictably, the excellent ones are all located in the capital cities; the abysmal ones in the far reaches of rural villages. Those attending the latter are usually ill-equipped for success.

Excerpts from Inward Hunger: The Education of a Prime Minister, the autobiography of Eric Williams, the late Prime Minister of Trinidad and Tobago, poignantly capture the formidable institutional obstacles encountered by the upwardly mobile ranks of the middle and lower classes. These are the words of a man who mastered the system, won the nation's highest educational award, the "Island Scholarship", and received his doctorate from Oxford University:

"The Government left education almost entirely in the hands of the Christian churches. Three enormous consequences followed from this abdication by the government of its

responsibility.   The first was the total
absence of uniformity in the school system. . .
in 1911, the attitude to secondary education
was inevitably ultra-conservative. There were
four secondary schools in the island.
Secondary education was exclusively urban. It
was also very expensive. Secondary education
was thus severely aristocratic. . .

The purpose of the secondary school in Trinidad
was to ensure the Anglicanization of the
colony. It consciously took the English public
school as its model. The external examinations
of Oxford and Cambridge, in which Trinidad was
the first colony to participate, strengthened
the prevailing English influence.

The secondary curriculum was indistinguishable
from that of an English public school.   The
standard of work in classics and mathematics
came in for high praise in 1911.   The good
students held their own with their colleagues
in England and the Empire. . . .

To what could a boy born in that year, the son
of a junior civil servant of the coloured lower
middle class, reasonably aspire, assuming he
had talent, "brains" to use the Trinidad
expression?

There were two openings - the civil service or
the professions. For the former a secondary
school education was desirable, for the latter
indispensable".

                         (Williams 1969:22-24).

It is undeniable that changes have taken place
in the social institutions of Trinidad and Tobago
since 1911. Even in the domain of education this
is so. There are now many secondary schools in the
island, although the top schools are the very same
four Williams mentioned. Secondary education is no

economy
unemployment

longer the prerogative of the upper classes, to the extent that it is now provided free of charge to all children of school age. The content of the secondary curriculum has been amended to include syllabi of relevance to the Caribbean. And, there is a university system in the region, making higher education attainable for some without having to go overseas, as was formerly necessary.

Nonetheless, it is possible to argue that the overall structure of the educational system has remained essentially intact (Hamid 1981:39). The English public school is still its model. British values and deportment are still emulated. Secondary school leaving examinations designed and evaluated by Cambridge University are still administered. Only very recently, in 1982, was there added a Caribbean analogue to the Cambridge examination system, on a trial basis. Most importantly, uniformity in the school system remains elusive and education of high quality remains exclusively urban. Tremendous impediments still block the path of the rural population in their quest for a decent education. Many parents residing in the countryside send their children to board in the city with relatives or family friends in order to attend a better school. Those children unable to board in the city must journey back and forth daily, spending a large portion of the day in travel alone.

In sum, there has been some change in the substance of the educational system, but there has certainly been no radical transformation in form or spirit. My personal observations during recent visits support this view. As Rubin and Zavalloni (1969) found in their study of school children of all social classes and ethnic backgrounds in Trinidad and Tobago, a strong "ethos of mobility" pervades children of the lower classes and lower segments of the middle class. Given the limitations just described, "the problem of opportunity becomes the crucial factor in the society" (Rubin & Zavalloni 1969:201).

CHAPTER III

PROFILE OF WEST INDIANS IN THE UNITED STATES,
NETWORK METHODOLOGY AND PROFILE OF
THE AFRO-TRINIDADIAN SAMPLE

DESCRIPTION OF THE WEST INDIAN IMMIGRANT POPULATION
IN THE UNITED STATES

It would appear, then, that a migratory ethos
has been etched into the West Indian psyche. The
term "West Indian" is used here to refer only to
the English-speaking Caribbean. Between 1965 and
1980, in the period following the Immigration and
Nationality Act of 1965, immigration from Jamaica
increased by 932.7 percent, while immigration from
Trinidad and Tobago increased 962.7 percent. It is
possible to obtain widely differing estimates of
the size of the West Indian population in the
United States depending on the source from which
the data are drawn. One source is based on
Immigration and Naturalization Service statistics
and relies on the numbers of West Indians who filed
Alien Address Reports for the year 1980. Another
source is the 1980 U.S. population census, in the
category of ancestry of population. The two
sources yield drastically different figures as
Table 2 shows.

The I.N.S. method of estimating the West Indian
immigrant population in the United States is
problematic for several reasons. In the first
place, many aliens do not file address reports
although they are required to do so by law. These

42

figures, then, are misleading in the sense that
they are an undercount, since they do not include
those who have not filed address reports. The most
important consideration, however, is that these
figures do not take into account the numbers of
West Indians in this country who are not
documented. The question of illegal immigration is
an important one. It is estimated that illegal
migration exceeds legal migration flows by two to
three times (Kritz 1981:218). Some estimates run
as high as five times the magnitude of documented
migration, but there are no reliable assessments
of volume or demographic characteristics (Kritz
1981). Given this situation, it is not really
possible to arrive at any exact figures.

A different method that may be more accurate,
but it is still subject to an undercount, is to
look at figures from the 1980 national population
census for the U.S. These figures, at least, are
not inherently skewed in favor of the legally
admitted population. Table 2 illustrates the
contrast between the two sources and makes the
undercount of the Immigration and Naturalization
Service figures quite apparent. Attention should
be drawn to the fact that even those figures from
the 1980 Census ought also to be considered an
underestimate because many undocumented migrants do
not fill out census questionnaires or any documents
that might reveal their presence in America.

The West Indian immigrant population is not
uniformly distributed throughout the United States.
Rather, West Indians have tended to concentrate in
the metropolitan centers of the East Coast. The
vast majority are located in the New York/New
Jersey area. Florida, particularly Miami and its
environs, has the second largest concentration.
This is followed by the combined populations of the
states of Massachusetts and Connecticut, the two
New England states where they congregate. There
are sizable numbers in the area of the nation's
capital, Washington D.C. and Maryland. Moreover,
quite a few are now located in the state of
California. Other states with fairly large numbers

of West Indians include Illinois, Michigan, Ohio,
Pennsylvania and Texas.

The sex ratio of the West Indian immigrant
population has swung from the extreme of males
outnumbering females, in the days when Ira de A.
Reid studied them, to the other extreme of females
outnumbering males. In the case of Jamaicans, the
ratio is almost 2:1; in the case of those from
Trinidad and Tobago and Barbados, there are 16%
more females; in the case of Guyanese, only 8% more
females. It should be pointed out, however, that
this is a function of family reunification, as the
numbers of housewives with no occupations has
increased dramatically.

In terms of age, the West Indian immigrant
population is relatively young. The majority are
in the 20-29 age range. There are also large
numbers in the 30-39 age range and a moderate
number in the 40-49 and 50-59 age ranges. The
numbers of those 60 years and older drop quite
dramatically. The sizable numbers who are age 15
years and under reflect the success of family
reunification policies, as these could not be
independent immigrants. These are the children of
previous migrants.

The occupational distribution of the West
Indian immigrant population is quite diverse. The
relatively large numbers who are housewives and
children again reflect family reunification
policies in action. There are impressive numbers
in the professional/technical and managerial/
administrative groups. However, the largest
numbers are in the clerical and service categories.
Workers in these categories would most likely be
required to have the equivalent of a high school
education. Those in the craft and operative
categories would need skills and training,
although of a different sort. The numbers in
domestic work are quite small compared with the
other categories. Data from the 1980 U.S. Census
on income distribution of the West Indian
population, including mean and median income, were
not yet available in published form at the time of

writing. As a result, they are not accessible for this analysis.

DESCRIPTION OF THE AFRO-TRINIDADIAN IMMIGRANT POPULATION IN LOS ANGELES

It has not been possible to get an accurate assessment of the size of the Afro-Trinidadian population in Los Angeles for several reasons. The figures from the Immigration and Naturalization Service do not contain information on a unit as small as a metropolitan area. Their smallest unit of data is a state. The figures from the U.S. Population Census 1980, based on the ancestry of the population, also contains information only about states. The figures from the 1980 Population Census based on the social and economic characteristics of the population in California, do break down into units of counties and metropolitan areas. However, these do not include the category Trinidadian.

The only West Indian population included in these figures is the category Jamaican. The numbers of Jamaicans living in the Standard Cosmopolitan Statistical Area that includes Los Angeles, Long Beach and the Anaheim area is 4,463. Assuming that there are three to four times as many Jamaican immigrants as there are Trinidadian ones, based on available data, it would be logical to infer that if there are 4,463 Jamaican immigrants in the Los Angeles Metropolitan area, then most likely there might be approximately 1,000 Trinidadian immigrants. Since it has not even been possible to assess the size of the Afro-Trinidadian population, it goes without saying that other demographic characteristics of population are not known.

THE CASE FOR SOCIAL NETWORK ANALYSIS

The concept of a social network as a set of ramifying social links between individuals has enjoyed metaphorical usage in social science for quite some time. Its analytical use, however, has been recent. The analytical use of social networks grew out of dissatisfaction with more static modes of traditional structural-functional analysis focussed on corporate groups and institutions (Barnes 1972; Mitchell 1974). It should be pointed out, however, that network analysis and institutional analysis are not competing models. Rather, network relationships and group structure operate on different levels of abstraction, and as such, ought to complement one another (Mitchell 1974; Whitten & Wolfe 1973). Moreover, network analysis remains grounded in basic ideas of structural-functional analysis except for the work of those who have chosen to anchor their analyses on Blauian exchange theory or on game theory (Whitten & Wolfe 1973).

The aim of social network analysis is to specify the sets of linkages among a defined set of persons and to use the characteristics of these links to explain the behavior of the individuals involved (Mitchell 1974). This sort of network analysis utilizes network morphology as a component of the theoretical model in which properties of networks are treated as independent variables that affect the behavior of individuals. For instance, Bott (1971) in her pioneering, and now famous, study of families in London, correlated the morphological characteristics of family networks, i.e., close-knit or loose-knit, with conjugal role behavior of spouses, i.e., segregated or joint.

Another study, more relevant to the research at hand, is Philip Mayer's (1961) analysis of divergences in network structure found in two different groups of migrants to a South African town. Observing that city life demands more acts of choice than country life, Mayer found an association between differences in network characteristics of the two migrant groups and the different rates at which they became absorbed into urban institutions (Mayer 1961).

The thrust of Mayer's study was to show how small size, density and multiplexity of social networks militate against assimilation into the mainstream of urban life, while large, loosely-connected and single-stranded (uniplex) networks favor it. In other words, close-knit networks, by fostering a sense of alienation, inhibit the integration of individuals into the wider social order, whereas loose-knit networks promote it via an elaborate communication system. Although hypothesis testing was not one of the initial aims of this research, Mayer's findings are germane to the population under study and are difficult to ignore. In particular, the migration of Afro-Trinidadians from New York City, where social networks are dense and close-knit (McLaughlin 1981), to Los Angeles where individuals are widely dispersed geographically and where the roles of kinsman, friend, neighbor and colleague seldom intersect, must be examined in light of the changes in the structure of their social networks accompanying this move.

Critics of network analysis have asserted that there is no such thing as network theory. If what they mean by this is a series of testable propositions or an over-arching theory, they are quite right. There is as yet little agreement on basic concepts, definitions and terminology. Those network analysts who concede that there is no network theory have chosen to adopt two theoretical bases as the most suitable for network analysis: interaction theory and exchange theory (Mitchell 1974). The goal of the interaction approach is to explain how norm-directed behavior is achieved by examining morphological and interactional characteristics of network links. The approach based on exchange theory assumes that individuals maintain network links for instrumental reasons and mobilize them for specific purposes. From this perspective, a social network may be a mechanism for distributing goods, services and information from person to person based on the concept of reciprocity. Whitten and Wolfe (1973) propose exchange theory as the most fertile theoretical foundation for network analysis.

A "total" social network is an infinite assemblage of social relations without boundaries in time or space. Consequently, analysts have had to set conceptual limits to networks to bring order into their analyses. With respect to size, the unit of analysis used in this study was the "personal" network or the series of links traced from an identified ego. This personal network was further subdivided into important zones within which social relations differed qualitatively. The intimate zone is composed of closest relatives and intimate friends. The effective zone consists of those relatives and friends with whom ego is on warm terms because they are important in the practical logistics of everyday life, i.e., instrumental friends and relatives. The extended zone is composed of those persons with whom he/she is barely acquainted, otherwise known as "friends of friends" (Boissevain 1974).

The time dimension is also one that must be limited in analyses, since total networks range, in principle, as far back into the past and as far forward into the future as the imagination will take you (Whitten & Wolfe 1973). Another consideration, if social network analysis is to meet its claim of superiority over the static, timeless quality of previous structural-functional analyses, is that it must incorporate into its framework the fact that social relations exist in time and change through time. Data collection in this study extended from September 1981 to March 1984, a period of two and a half years. Efforts were made to document changes in social networks and social interaction occurring over this period. As it was not logistically possible to visit all participants in their homes frequently, one particularly successful method of documenting change over time was participation by me in "gossip" networks of which I am a member.

The term "gossip" is not used here in its pejorative sense of "badmouth" or "badtalk," or in the sense of meddling in other people's affairs. Rather, "gossip" is used here to refer to what Trinidadians call "oletalk," which is a verbal exchange between two or more persons either on the telephone or in face-to-face gatherings during which they chat casually about what is happening in each other's personal lives and in the lives of other people they know.

This type of interaction has been described by Hannerz (1967) as "gossip," which he regards as a way of getting information about others that allows one to construct a detailed map of one's social environment. The information may or may not be judgmental or pejorative. This method of acquiring information is especially useful, in Hannerz' view, in communities of loose-knit networks with low interaction frequencies, in which there may be a lengthy time lapse in the interaction of two specified persons. If there is a link in common to both, the link can keep them both up to date on what has happened with each one through "gossip" (Hannerz 1967). Participation by me in telephone conversations consisting of "oletalk" that took place from time to time over the period of data collection, was the most successful way to keep abreast of what was going on in the lives of network members. It was also a very effective way to inject time depth into the analysis.

"Oletalk" can occur either on the telephone or in face-to-face encounters. Apart from telephone conversations, part of the research design entailed intermittent participation in private parties at the homes of the participants, in dances at West Indian night clubs, in public dances sponsored by organized West Indian groups, and in "liming" (American equivalent = hanging out) in a Trinidadian restaurant whose owner is a close friend. Settings in which I did not participate or observe were the soccer and cricket matches that some West Indians engage in regularly. During the course of these casual, relaxed encounters with participants and their friends in these recreational settings, it became evident through participant observation, that these contexts are some of the ones in which Afro-Trinidadians keep informed, via face-to-face "oletalk," of other Afro-Trinidadians who are not in the intimate zone of their networks, but are in the effective and extended zones. It was a perfect opportunity for me to do the same.

Although there is agreement that both structural and interactional criteria should be used in examining linkages between persons, there is no analytical concensus on precise measures to be used. For this reason, certain morphological and interactional characteristics that seemed relevant to this research were chosen to be used in the study.

The following structural features of personal networks were assessed:

1) Size -- the actual number of persons in the network, both kin and friends.
2) Range -- the type of relationships or composition of networks.
3) Density -- the extent to which those persons linked to an ego are also linked to one another.
4) Clustering -- the segments of networks with high density, often recruited out of different activity fields. Alternatively conceptualized as the density of different segments of a personal network.
5) Intimate Zone - that composed of both kin and friends who are on the closest of terms.
6) Effective Zone - that composed of kin and friends with whom one has warm relations for strategic purposes, i.e., instrumental kin and friends.
7) Extended Zone - that composed of mere acquaintances, i.e., friends of friends.

The interactional content of networks was also investigated, in particular the following:

1) Multiplexity -- the extent to which a network link involves multiple role relationships, i.e., more than one focus of interaction (uniplex), and has several overlapping contents. Network analysts believe multiplex relationships to be more binding than uniplex ones.

2) Normative content -- the nature of the links in a network may be distinguished by content such as kinship, friendship, occupation, ethnicity, race, neighborhood, etc. In this study, special attention was paid to kin-based vs. friend-based content.

3) Transactional content -- the nature of the items exchanged in interaction, for example, letters, money, gifts, telephone calls, visits, being a house guest, children living as guests, babysitting, parties.

4) Intensity -- the evaluation of network links in terms of the emotional value attached to the relationship, not necessarily dependent on face-to-face or frequent interaction. This is particularly true of immigrant ties with their homeland.

5) Frequency -- the frequency of interaction.

6) Durability -- the length of time of the relationship.

A DEMOGRAPHIC PROFILE OF THE AFRO-TRINIDADIAN SAMPLE

The sample is equally divided in terms of gender, consisting of fifteen male and fifteen female participants (see Table 3). All thirty participants were born in Trinidad (see Table 3). Male participants range in age from 25 to 68 years old and female participants from 29 to 48 years old. With respect to marital status, more than half of the males (53%) and females (67%) are married. Twenty percent of the females and thirty-three percent of the males are divorced. Only one male and one female are co-habiting. Only one male and one female are single and have never been married (see Table 3). Attention should be drawn to the fact that the marital status of four of the participants changed several times during the course of research, a fact that is not reflected in the static classification of Table 3, which is valid only for 1984. One male participant was married in 1981, separated in 1982, got divorced in 1983 and remains so in 1984. One female was divorced during 1981 and 1982, remarried in 1983 and is still married in 1984. Those in the categories of single and cohabiting have not changed their statuses during the course of research.

Divergences in the sample between males and females are quite evident in their educational attainment levels. It can be seen from Table 4 that all males and all females completed their primary school education. However, whereas all females also completed secondary school, only 60% of the males did. Six of the males (40%) who did not finish secondary school, plus one of the males (6.6%) who did, went on to train at technical institutes to "learn a trade," as they put it. After completing their secondary school education, six of the females (40%) also went further for additional training in such areas as clerical and secretarial work, bookkeeping and keypunch operating (see Table 4). Three of the females (20%) went on to attend university but did not complete their degrees. Eight of the males (53%) and five of the females (33%) who also went on to university managed to obtain their Bachelor's degrees. Three of the males (20%) are currently engaged in post-graduate course work, while two of them (13%) have attained Master's degrees. Four of the males (26%) have finished professional school (one medical doctor, one accountant and two

engineers), while five of the females (33%) have
completed their nurses' training (see Table 4).

With regard to occupation, one third of the
women are professionals, while a little over one
quarter of the men are. Three of the men (20%)
and three of the women (20%) are in management/
administration. However, women (40%) predominate
in clerical work, only one male being in that
line, while men (40%) predominate in the skilled
crafts domain. Only one person, who is male, is in
sales, and only one person, who is female, is a
full-time student (see Table 5). One of the males
in the management category is actually a
multi-millionaire real estate investor.

The employment history of the Afro-Trinidadian
sample was also analysed for the years 1981, 1982,
1983, and 1984 in order to draw attention to
changes occurring over this period. It should be
noted that very few changes have occurred in the
employment patterns of females. Fourteen of the
females (93%) had secure employment in 1981 and
1982. During this time, only one woman, the
full-time student was marginally employed because
she worked part-time. In 1983, one woman who had
previously been securely employed became marginally
employed. In 1984, she resumed secure employment,
bringing the 1984 pattern for women back to its
former state in 1981 and 1982.

For the men, however, the picture is quite
different. The employment status of one male, the
68 year old retired medical doctor, did not change
during the course of research. This was the only
exception. In 1981, only ten (66%) of the males
were securely employed, while four of them (26%)
were marginally employed. In 1982, things became
worse: six of the men (40%) were not employed at
all, while only eight of them (53%) remained
securely employed, although none were marginally
employed. Of the six men who were unemployed in
1982, one was professional, one was in sales and
four of them were skilled manual workers. In 1983,
nine men (60%) were securely employed, two men
(13%) were marginally employed and three men (20%)

were not employed at all. The two men marginally
employed are skilled craftsmen. Of the three men
unemployed, one is in management, the other two are
skilled craftsmen. The picture for 1984 has
brightened only slightly: nine men (60%) remain
securely employed, four (26%) are only marginally
employed, but only one (6.6%) is unemployed. The
lone unemployed male is a skilled craftsman
belonging to an union. One of the four marginally
employed is in management.

Two insights may be gained from the employment
patterns described above for male members of the
sample. One is that blue-collar workers who are
male and black are extremely susceptible to being
laid off. As others have observed, they are the
last to be hired and the first to be fired.
Particularly during economically lean times such as
the recent recession, many are only able to obtain
irregular work on an intermittent basis. This is
true in spite of membership in an union. Another
lesson to be learned is that white-collar managers,
if black and male, also succomb to unemployment.
In short, white-collar status does not lessen the
vulnerability of the black male to unemployment.

Two other variables considered significant in
affecting immigrant assimilation are length of
residence in the United States, and in this case,
length of residence in Los Angeles as well. Length
of residence in the United States ranged from six
years to 40 years for males and from three years to
twenty years for females, in the sample. Length of
residence in Los Angeles ranged from three years to
twenty-nine years for men and from three years to
nineteen years for women. Two men lived briefly in
Puerto Rico. They stated it was because Puerto
Rico is "the back door" to the United States (a
euphemism for illegal entry into the U.S.). Two
other men and one woman lived in the U.S. Virgin
Islands for two to six years. The two men (two
skilled craftsmen) migrated there because they
learned of job opportunities. The woman had
accompanied her parents there as a young girl. One
woman spent two years in England furthering her

studies, another spent twenty-two years there. The latter initially attended boarding school there, then pursued her nurse's training there and later practiced nursing in England before coming to Los Angeles.

A considerable proportion of the sample lived in the New York/New Jersey area and other Eastern cities for one to ten years prior to migrating to Los Angeles: ten men (66%) and ten women (66%). Contrasts between New York and Los Angeles in terms of the structure of social networks of Afro-Trinidadians will rely heavily on the testimony of these individuals and partly on the research findings of other scholars who have studied West Indians in New York, e.g., McLaughlin (1981).

Relationships between the variables of geographical mobility, age, marital status, employment status and occupation were also analysed. A clear linear relationship between age and length of residence in the United States among male sample members was observed. In contrast to males under age 40, those aged 40 and above have lived in Los Angeles for a much longer period. Also, more of the males under age 40 have moved to Los Angeles from the East than those above age 40.

With respect to marriage, in all age groups except for the under 30 category, male participants tend to be married. Males who are divorced tend to be aged 40 and above. Among female sample members, there is no female representation in the 50-69 age range. More importantly, female participants have been U.S. residents for less time than males. More females than males have moved from the East to Los Angeles. More female sample members are married than males (two-thirds female vs. one half males). Also, divorced females are concentrated in the early thirties age range whereas divorced males tend to be aged 50 and above.

As far as the variable of employment status is concerned, the unemployment rate for male participants was exceptionally high in 1982. Except for the retired male in his sixties, and males in their forties, all other age categories were affected by unemployment. In other words, the relationship between age and unemployment is not a linear one. Neither is the relationship between length of residence and unemployment a strong one. Males who have been in the United States for twenty-five years and those who have only been in the country for a few years, alike, were victims of unemployment in 1982.

However, marginal employment among males, over the four year period 1981-1984, appears to be related to age to the extent that younger men in their twenties and thirties were more vulnerable, although one male in his forties was also vulnerable. Marginal employment does not appear to be related to length of residence among male participants. During the period 1981-1984, most males were securely employed, the year 1982 being anomalous. Over the four year period, there were four male sample members, however, who were exceptional in consistently alternating between marginal employment and complete unemployment.

The employment patterns of the female sample contrast dramatically with that of the male participants. Over the four year period 1981-1984, the vast majority of females were securely employed, unlike their male counterparts. The only consistent exception was a young woman in her twenties who was marginally employed over the four years because of her student status. One other woman in her early thirties was marginally employed only during 1983. The categories of retired and unemployed are non-existent for females. There is no clear relationship between age, length of residence and employment status for female participants.

Since there was virtually no change in patterns of employment over the four year period for women, the relationship between occupation and employment status was only explored for male participants for the year 1982. In 1982, at least one unemployed male in each of the five occupational categories was noted. In other words, as far as male sample

members were concerned, it did not matter whether
their occupation was of high or low rank, all males
were susceptible to unemployment.   Conversely,
female participants were securely employed, for the
most part, between 1981-1984 regardless of their
occupational rank.   Put differently, there appears
to be no strong relationship between occupational
status and employment status.   Similarly, there is
no clear relationship between level of education
attained and security of employment.

CHAPTER IV

MIGRATION PROCESSES

This chapter details the processes by means of which sample members migrated to the United States. Chain migration appears to be the dominant pattern, based on the activation of primary relationships, with kinship and friendship relations most salient. Kinship and friendship networks are vital for mediating the move and the initial settlement. Family re-unification and social mobility are among the most important motives for migration, seeking adventure ranking third. The twin benefits of a mild, pleasant climate and kin/friends to receive them drew participants to Los Angeles from other North American cities. Others were drawn by specialized training that could only be obtained in Los Angeles for particular occupations such as aerospece engineering or the entertainment industry. Some also came to Los Angeles because they considered Los Angeles a better environment in which to raise children.

MIGRATION MOTIVES OF THE AFRO-TRINIDADIAN SAMPLE

As one might expect, just under half (47%) of the participants had multiple reasons. I shall deal only with primary motives. Primary motives can be classified into three general categories: 1) kinship, 2) social mobility, and 3) seeking adventure. Analysis of these motives yielded two striking observations. One is that social mobility is of overriding importance, as a primary motive for both men and women. The other is that kinship considerations are important for both sexes.

With respect to kinship, without question the most common motive among the participants was that of joining one's parent(s). Over a quarter of the sample migrated to the United States mainly for this reason. The case of Yvette Harris is instructive:

"Mummy went to New York first. . .She came up on a visitor's visa and then this lady sponsored her. . .Since she was a child, Mummy always had a passion to go to the States, so when the opportunity came, she grabbed it. She didn't want the family to be split up, so she decided that we should join her. She was in New York for about a year before we went. We stayed in Trinidad. Our visas came through. She went by herself first, but nobody wanted to go. . .We didn't want to come. There are five of us, me, two brothers and two sisters. . . (When we came) we didn't want to stay, life was nice in Trinidad..... We stayed because Mummy insisted and cried. . .Mummy insisted that the whole family stay together. . .We used to stay with an Aunt because Mummy couldn't find an apartment big enough for all of us. She couldn't find a three bedroom apartment in Brooklyn. So we stayed with this Aunt, all in one bedroom and it was miserable. At that time it was hard to find an apartment, you were forced to buy a house. Fortunately, everybody was working, so Daddy ran a family "susu".[1] In three months we bought a house. Everybody just pooled together for a down payment."

Yvette's account deserves attention for several reasons. First of all, it attests to the dedication and drive that spurs some individuals, in this instance Yvette's mother, to pursue a life-long ambition to emigrate and to leap at the opportunity when it comes their way. Often, it is a path fraught with uncertainty. For instance, she migrated on a visitor's visa (as a tourist) on the chance that she would find sponsorship by an American family, most likely as a domestic. She was fortunate enough to be sponsored, as many others simply overstay their tourist visas and become illegal immigrants. Secondly, it is indicative of a common pattern of chain migration by which most New Immigrants arrive in this country. In this case, Yvette's father and brothers and sisters were sent for by her mother when her immigration status was settled. Lastly, it underscores the importance of the family to the New Immigrants. Yvette's mother insisted on keeping the family together, despite many obstacles. It is also worth noting that Yvette and family were provided with lodging by a relative until such time as they were able to make better living arrangements for themselves. They did so by pooling together their finances in a rotating credit association, limited to family members only, so that they might live more comfortably. The sharing of resources for living by family members and relatives seems to be a common modus vivendi among West Indians in New York (see McLaughlin 1981).

Again, kinship appears to be crucial to the migration process. If one's ambition is to go to the United States, then joining one's siblings already there is another way to do it. Bert Diamond did precisely that:

"As a kid growing up, my goals and plans were always to go to the United States. My brothers and sisters were all out here and they were doing fairly well. It was always my aspiration to come to the States. . .I am the youngest. I

am the last of thirteen. When I graduated from
high school, I started to work for what was
then British Petroleum and I stayed there for
about three years. They had a major strike in
1963. . .I decided to. . .leave for the United
States. I passed through New York on my way to
Los Angeles. I stayed there a couple of months
with one of my sisters who was living there at
the time. She's living here now."

Earlier it was pointed out that occupational
self-improvement was a major consideration in
migration. In fact, the second most common motive
for emigration appears to be to further one's
education. It will be recalled that in Chapter II,
I suggested that "educational opportunities and
life chances were rigidly circumscribed" (Rubin &
Zavalloni 1969) for a large number of Afro-
Trinidadians. At the same time, they are imbued
with an "ethos of mobility" (Rubin & Zavalloni
1969). Almost half of the sample admitted to
leaving Trinidad because of institutional barriers
blocking them from certain life-goals. This
finding provides empirical support for the limited
educational and occupational opportunity
hypothesis.

Consider, for example, the fact that out of
thirty individuals, only three men and one woman
(13%) attended the highest ranked secondary schools
in the island. There are only four secondary
schools considered to be top in the nation, all of
them being in the capital city of Port of Spain.
They are St. Mary's College and Queen's Royal
College for boys and St. Joseph's Convent and
Bishop Anstey High School for girls. Co-education
does not exist at the secondary level in Trinidad.
Attendance at one of these four schools is
practically de rigueur to be accepted into a
British university or technical institute. As one
male participant put it:

"Opportunities for further education were limited unless you went to Queen's Royal College or St. Mary's. . .you couldn't get in."

However, mere attendance at one of the "big four" secondary schools does not guarantee admission into British higher education. Outstanding performance in the Cambridge school leaving examinations is necessary to qualify. Since students at the top schools have always been encouraged to go to the U.K., the "mother country," the choice of the U.S. made by the three men and the woman indicates that they found the U.S. more attractive for one or more reasons. In some ways this is surprising because "the old English thing is still there," as one individual put it. As another participant reports:

"Our system is so English-oriented that we don't recognize diplomas and stuff from this part of the world (the U.S.A.). I think it still exists, that English bias. You remember when doctors trained in the States would not have their degrees recognized unless they went to Canada or the U.K. to take their exams and be certified? I don't think the American influence is so great yet. Well, actually, it has changed some. For instance, I see some scholarships offered to American universities, I don't know in what areas. And some of those winning Island Scholarships are choosing to come to the States."

One of the three men explained what he found more attractive about the United States when he came here to attend medical school:

"What made me come to the States instead of going to England was that my father was very poor. He was a schoolmaster and made about sixteen dollars a month in those days. I knew that I could work here part-time and during the summertime, which I did. You can't do that in England."

Indeed, the American educational system has an added appeal for many Afro-Trinidadians precisely because it is structured in such a way that it is possible for students to study and work at the same time. In contrast, the system of higher education in Britain effectively prohibits any sort of work/study agenda. Only those who have the financial means to cover all living and educational expenses for the duration of study, either from a scholarship or from personal sources, can expect a chance at higher education in the British system. Those without such resources, in effect, have little choice but to come to the U.S. The four individuals in question appear to have profited from their American experience, for the three men are now professionals and the woman is just finishing up her college education. Ian Nelson, one of the three men, accounted for his decision to come to the United States in this way:

"The reason why I came to the States was to enhance my ability and to progress. At that time, Trinidad was under British rule and it was hard to progress in Trinidad, although I had a good education. I went to St. Mary's. I was working a few different jobs in Trinidad. . .I went as far as School Certificate, then I went out to work. [School Certificate is the old terminology that is the equivalent of G.C.E. Ordinary Levels, which is insufficient for admission into a British university. Advanced Levels is required]. My first job was at the Ministry of Works. . .Trinidad wasn't industrialized as it is now. Trying to move up in various jobs at that time was very hard, so I decided the thing for me to do was for me to leave the country. I had a choice between the U.S. and the U.K. I chose the U.S. because I thought it was easier, England had more restrictions."

Education may also be circumscribed for distinctively female reasons, as reported by Jeanette Edwards:

"I was one of these unfortunate kids that got pregnant in school at sixteen years old. You know when you get pregnant back home, you cannot go to school anymore. So I felt if I stayed in Trinidad, I would have been there and had at least fifteen kids or more and minding animals and stuff and I wouldn't have a chance to do anything more in life, because when you have a kid there, that's it, your school days are over. So I thought if I went to the Virgin Islands I would be able to do something with myself instead of sitting around, so I took my mother's offer. My mother, me, three sisters and one brother. My father is in the Virgin Islands also and my mother still lives there. . I know if I was back in Trinidad I wouldn't be doing this good. Here, all you need is a high school diploma to get your foot in the door. In order to improve, you have to continue school to get further up. But in this country, you can keep going to school all the time if you want, which I love. And if you want to really improve, you keep doing it. But back home, you have to have G.C.E. O levels and A Levels before you could get anyplace. If I was back home, nobody would hire me in a bank."

In other words, had Jeanette not left Trinidad, she would not have had a chance to finish her secondary education or acquire additional training, and she would never have qualified for the responsible, white-collar job she holds today as Assistant Supervisor in the Collections Department of a bank.

Based on Jeanette's experience, it is clear that a far worse handicap, in the Trinidadian context, than a second-rate or third-rate education is an incomplete one. It will be recalled that six men (20%) did not finish secondary school in

Trinidad, dropping out around age thirteen or
fourteen. Such an act has dire consequences in a
system that furnishes no second chances. Had these
men remained in Trinidad, they would most likely
have been condemned to roaming from one unskilled
job to another for the rest of their days. As it
turned out, five of the men were able to enroll in
trade schools in the U.S. and to acquire a skill
and to become steadily employed until the recent
recession which hurt them quite badly. The sixth
man, Colin Dexter, has fulfilled the classic
American dream. His "rags to riches" tale begins
this way:

> "I came to the States to better my life, to
> improve myself. There's no future for a young
> person in Trinidad. I left Trinidad when I was
> 17 years old. I was working for Leaseholds
> (large company) as an office boy. My mother
> has no formal education. . .My father was the
> manager of W. Thomas and Co. He worked there
> for thirty years. In those days, you didn't
> have nobody dark-skinned managing no firm.
> They fired him for giving an Indian man a piece
> of rope and left my mother with nothing, not a
> dime. So I told myself, never happen to me. I
> am going to be in control of my destiny."

Colin Dexter then proceeded to "escape from
Trinidad to come to the United States." He worked
on farms picking strawberries, peas and corn. Then
he moved to New York to be with his grandfather.
He spent two years there working in factories. But
he didn't care for the cold and moved to California
where two uncles and his grandmother lived. In Los
Angeles he enrolled in high school, got his diploma
and went on to college, all the while working odd
jobs such as washing cars and being a janitor.
After finishing his Bachelor's degree, he went to
work for a large insurance company and became
interested in Liability. This inspired him to take
courses at a small law school and eventually he
went to work for a law firm. There he got exposed

to the world of real estate. When he came to the
realization that working for other people had no
value at all, he decided to co-invest with a friend
in a piece of property in a wealthy neighborhood.
Within less than a year he had more than doubled
his money. From then on he has been dealing in
real estate and investments and today the man is a
multi-millionaire.

Naturally, not everyone is dealt the same cards
as Colin Dexter. Others, like him, who did not
complete their secondary education in Trinidad,
have not been blessed with his good fortune. Take
Malcolm Williams, for example. He left school at
age thirteen because his teachers treated him badly
and humiliated him. For a while he tried going to
trade school but he got discouraged there also and
left. For the next three years he worked as a
seasonal laborer on sugar cane estates, baling
cane. He left that job for one in a detergent
factory which lasted five months. His family moved
to another town where he was able to pick up some
welding skills from friends. But, he still could
not find steady work anywhere in Trinidad. So he
decided to leave the country, thinking he would
have better luck abroad. During his sixteen years
of residence in the United States he has drifted
from job to job, mostly in factories, except for a
period from 1977 to 1982, when he was steadily
employed as a welder and making a decent wage.
From 1981 on he has only had sporadic employment.
Much of his life in America has consisted of
unemployment. In frustration, he decided to
return to Trinidad in December 1983 because his
parents had found work for him there.

Some of the participants made the move to the
United States when they recognized that the
possibilities for occupational advancement were
extremely limited. One such participant was
Roderick Philips, a former schoolteacher in
Trinidad. He could see stagnation approaching as
he taught the same forms year after year. On
reflection, he knew he would not make Principal as
there were too many senior teachers above him. So,

after completing his three year contract of
Government Service required of teachers trained in
government teaching colleges, he left Trinidad for
New York in order to change careers. Before
leaving Trinidad, he had been informed that there
was a need for academic counselors, so he chose
Guidance and Counseling, believing it to be a good
field, and left with the intention of returning.
All through his training he was told there was a
continuing need for his new skills. After
completing his Bachelor's and Master's degrees at
Brooklyn College, he returned to Trinidad but met
only with frustration. No one paid him any
interest and it took much effort to find out what
his classification would be. Finally, he
discovered he would be making the same salary he
would have made, had he stayed on as a teacher. He
returned to New York and worked as a counselor at
Long Island University for four years before moving
to Los Angeles.

THE CHAIN MIGRATION PROCESS

It was alluded to earlier that Afro-
Trinidadians tend to come to the United States via
a specific mechanism: chain migration. Actually,
the process by means of which both New Immigrants
and Old Immigrants have typically moved from one
location to another, has been through chain
migration. In what is now considered to be a
classic in migration studies, MacDonald and
MacDonald (1964) analyzed the large-scale migration
process of Italian immigrants to the United States
at the turn of the century and found that it
followed the configuration of a "chain." They
defined chain migration as, "that movement in
which prospective migrants learn of opportunities,
are provided with transportation, and have initial
accommodation and employment arranged by means of
primary social relationships with previous

migrants" (MacDonald & MacDonald 1964:82). Apart
from identifying chain migration as a major type of
migratory pattern, the MacDonalds' main
contribution lies in the insight that
comprehending the organizing principles of any
migratory pattern and its historical context is
central to the understanding of the consequences of
migration and patterns of settlement and
adaptation (MacDonald & MacDonald 1964:84).

A case in point is the MacDonalds' (1964)
analysis of the patterns of settlement and
occupational adaptation of Italian immigrants to
the United States at the turn of the century. They
showed that these patterns were only partly
affected by American legislation, but were largely
determined by the internal dynamics of chain
migration based on kinship and patron-client
relationships, as opposed to "impersonally
organized migration." Why migrants came from
certain parts of Italy and why they settled only in
"Little Italies" of the U.S. remained a mystery
without an understanding of the kinship ties
linking certain towns in Italy with particular
communities in the U.S. Knowledge of the "padroni
system" in the U.S. which furnished accommodations
and employment was also indispensable to this
explanation. U.S. migration policy represented
only the "external" constraints within which this
"internal" system of sponsorship operated
(MacDonald & MacDonald 1964:82-91).

Most definitely, Afro-Trinidadian immigration
to the United States may be characterized as chain
migration. As previously observed, kinship plays a
critical role in this process. More importantly,
the sponsorship of prospective immigrants is
permitted by U.S. immigration law solely on the
basis of kinship. However close the friendship,
friends do not qualify as lawful sponsors. By
definition, therefore, chain migration is limited
exclusively to the category of kinsmen. Indeed, 63
percent of the Afro-Trinidadian sample (nineteen
individuals) migrated specifically to join close
family members already present in the United States

(see Table 6). These individuals were sponsored by nuclear family members.

What is worth noting, however, is that most of the remaining sample members, who did not come to the U.S. primarily for family reunification, upon their arrival, also had recourse to kin and friends as sources of support. On perusing Table 6, it is immediately apparent that a large number, twenty-five, of the participants (83%) were able to call upon primary relationships with previous migrants to assist them with the process of migration and with their initial adjustment upon arrival in this country. Seven men and five women were assisted by their parent(s). One man was assisted by a brother. One man was assisted by an uncle and two women were assisted by their aunts. One man by a cousin. That godparenting is still a viable institution in Trinidad, a predominantly Roman Catholic country, is attested to by the fact that one woman was aided by her godmother. Fictive kinship is also very much alive, as one woman received help from a fictive "cousin." Last but not least, friends were instrumental in assisting with migration as well, as experienced by two men and four women. Only five (17%) of the participants did not have their migration mediated by primary relationships: two men were sponsored by technical colleges as students, one entirely on his own, and two women sponsored by American families to work for them as domestics (see Table 6). In other words, the Afro-Trinidadian participants conform well with the MacDonalds' definition of chain migrants in that they learned of opportunities, were provided with their passage and had initial accommodation arranged through primary relationships with previous migrants.

One of the participants, Roderick Philips, whose migration history was detailed earlier, himself articulated the chain-like pattern that characterizes the process by which most Afro-Trinidadians arrive in this country:

"This is one of the points that might be of
interest to you in your research. Some friend
(or relative) would encourage someone back
home, either through letters or phone calls or
something, come up and check out the place.
So, Jean (his cousin) was always the one to
encourage me to come up and further my studies
up here. Perhaps she encouraged Margaret (his
wife) to come up also, because I tell you, from
that batch of nurses, who was the first to come
up? . . ..One person in that group, right?
Would come and would do well and that person
would write back and tell and encourage
others. They would come on vacation first.
Most of them came on vacation first. And then,
slowly, one by one would start coming. And I
think from their batch (of nurses) from 1964,
only one person is back home. One out of about
seventeen? So this is how Uncle Sam gets a lot
of professionals. Another thing, in terms of
the attraction for professional people, apart
from encouragement, when they come and see the
opportunities here, they lock out (of)
professional advancement home. . .Similarly for
another group of professionals, teachers, I was
a teacher back home. I had a fellow teacher,
he's in Canada now, he was the one who would
keep up correspondence and encourage me to
come. And it's like a chain reaction, because
when I came, I did the same thing for my
room-mate who is now in Albany. I don't know
who he did it for, but if you check up on
graduating groups of professionals. . .you
would see a pattern of the younger people
coming away, first on vacation and seeing the
educational opportunities and that would be
offset by the stagnation in their positions
back home, so they have this push to come
away."

Migration chains are based on the idea that, as
one moves, others follow. Marilyn Price, one of
the participants, described how it worked for her:

"I decided to come to the States because of my
family. My sister [oldest] was here. She had
been here for a long time. She filed my
mother's papers and they asked my mother who
she would like to take along. She said, my
brother, my sister and myself. So we came. .
I came up to the States with my mother. She
was the main person to come up first. She
brought three of us and left three girls back
home. Altogether it's eight of us in the
family. The three sisters followed later on."

Another participant, Maureen Sinclair,
described her family chain in this way:

"I have three brothers, they're all living here
now. . .....I sponsored my mother after I got
settled here. . ...My mother sponsored my
brothers one at a time, until they all got
here."

Yet another participant Heather Johnson,
recounted another kinship chain:

"I brought up my Mom and she sponsored one of
my brothers. My other brother went to Canada.
I snuck him through the border, I drove up to
Toronto and snuck him there. He's now married
to an American girl and got his papers
straightened out. He lives in Brooklyn now."

Afro-Trinidadians in particular, and West
Indians generally, are not unique in the practice
of chain migration. Kinship chains have been
documented by scholars for both Old and New
immigrant populations in the United States. With
respect to the New Immigration, policies in the
United States have shaped the form and content of
migration and settlement. The liberalizing of
immigration policy in the post-1965 period has
fostered the formation of kinship chains by
permitting the sponsorship of more categories of
kin than ever.

Among those to have established an unbroken chain of migration based on kinship, in the post-1965 era, have been the Chinese (Li 1977). Following almost a century of exclusion subsequent to the passage of the Anti-Chinese Exclusion Act of 1882, many Chinese families availed themselves of the change of heart in immigration law in 1965 by making use of kinship ties with previous Chinese immigrants. By alternately taking advantage of both consanguineal and affinal relationships, the Chinese have been extremely successful at manipulating these bonds to overcome institutional obstacles to immigration (Li 1977:59). This is possible, as Li observes, because kinship ties have a certain fluidity to them in that they may be formed in a variety of ways, i.e., by birth, marriage or fictive links. This suggests a variety of ways that they may be used to one's advantage. Accordingly, Li argues compellingly that kinship formation and maintenance should be treated most profitably as a resource-mobilizing mechanism, to cope with social structural constraints in the receiving country (Li 1977:61).

Based on the Afro-Trinidadian experience, it is being suggested here that Caribbean migrants, as a group, have been equally successful at this type of resource-mobilization in their move to America. Seventeen individuals (57%) had kinfolk mediating their migration and providing a reception for them. Two individuals had fictive kin doing the same thing, and six (20%) of them had close friends to receive them. Only five sample members (17%) had neither kin nor friends waiting for them on their arrival. Kinship networks, then, are vital components of a social structure that creates linkages between migrant and the receiving community, before the move, during the actual move and during initial settlement in the country of destination (Choldin 1973). They do so by functioning as a system of dissemination for migration information prior to the move and by providing assistance during the move itself, as well as during the settlement process (Choldin

1973).   In this way, migration re-establishes
social ties between individuals in a new community
and those from the homeland (Choldin 1973).

PRIMARY MIGRATION TO LOS ANGELES

What brought the members of the Afro-
Trinidadian sample to Los Angeles? The responses
to this question varied according to whether
participants were primary or secondary migrants to
Los Angeles, which is to say, whether they had come
directly from Trinidad or whether they had moved
here secondarily from the East coast and
elsewhere. Ten of the participants were primary
migrants and twenty of them secondary migrants.
Although many of the categories of motives for
coming to Los Angeles were shared by both primary
and secondary migrants, it is nevertheless useful
to distinguish these two types of migrants to L.A.
in order to acquire a better sense of what
particular conditions exist in Los Angeles that
attract Afro-Trinidadians enough to bring them here
from other metropolitan centers of the country and
how the two experiences differ. In addition, the
distinction ought to provide some insights into the
nature of the changes in patterns of social
organization resulting from secondary migration
from urban centers where social networks are dense
and close-knit, to the Los Angeles metropolitan
area where individuals are compelled to be widely
dispersed geographically. The outcome of such
geographical dispersion has often assumed the form
of structural and functional differentiation of
various types of primary groups like kin, friends
and neighbors (Litwak & Szelenyi 1969), chiefly
because these roles no longer intersect.
     Let us consider first, primary migration to Los
Angeles. Recruitment by kin, fictive kin, spouse
and friends, once again, plays a major role in
migration. It could certainly be suggested that

chain migration based on primary relationships was
operating here once more. The information network
system also appears to be functioning very well,
since a large number of participants found out
about the warm climate in California, mainly
through primary relationships. As in migration to
the United States generally, some primary migrants
to Los Angeles also decided to come here to improve
their skills and to further their education. One
individual came to learn a trade, specifically
auto-body repair, which he had wanted to learn in
Trinidad, but had left school at age thirteen and
had been forced to seek unskilled work in factories
instead. Five persons, four men and one woman,
came because they had been accepted by colleges in
Los Angeles. Three of these five also had kin,
fictive kin and friends to receive them. Only two
of these five had no primary group connections
prior to coming here. One of them, Kenneth
Simpson, related how he got here:

> "I didn't know a soul when I came to Los
> Angeles. I found out about aviation schools
> through books that I used to read at the U.S.
> Consulate, in their U.S.I.S. Library. I used
> to go there and read all the time. I applied
> to about four or five aviation schools and I
> chose California because it was supposed to be
> warm. I didn't want to be in the snow. I
> didn't really understand how far away Los
> Angeles was. In fact, that morning I left
> Trinidad, it was a scary feeling because I had
> no idea when I would be coming home again."

Lastly, one primary migrant, Gemma Jones gave a
reason not mentioned by anyone else, that she had
come here to change careers, more specifically, to
one in the music and entertainment industry. This
made a lot of sense since Los Angeles is the hub
of the music, television and motion picture
industries and there is probably no place better
suited to such aspirations. This is how she

explained the importance of Los Angeles for her future plans:

"I came up here to do recording engineering, that was my primary thing. . . I'm also doing video, television arts and sciences. . . The entertainment industry always fascinated me and I wanted to get into it through one or the other program. Music is my thing, as you can see from all the musical instruments around here. . . ..I like the States so far. I would like to stay and find some way to get my green card. I would like to get some working experience here. Eventually, what I'd like to do is to be able to go back and forth between here and Trinidad, because there are some projects I would like to develop in Trinidad. If I can get the money together, I would like to buy a set of video equipment. I would like to see if I could develop some educational programs too and maybe some kind of "sit-com" series. There are some quite good actors and actresses down in Trinidad who don't get a chance to show their talent. And all the programming on Trinidadian TV is foreign. And old imported stuff, too!"

The case of Gemma Jones draws attention to several observations. On a personal level, it is interesting to note her patriotic anxiety about imported fare on television in Trinidad. In fact, television programs in Trinidad do consist mainly of old re-runs of American programs. Her concern is great enough to prompt her to create serious alternatives. On a less individual level, however, it is noteworthy that her ultimate goal is to be able to travel back and forth between Los Angeles and Trinidad. In other words, she wants to become an "international shuttler." A growing number of the New Immigrants have become "international shuttlers." In the course of redefining a new modus vivendi that involves shifting residences as well as maintaining

loyalties and ties in more than one place, these
individuals highlight the need for rethinking the
concept of migration as a shift in the permanent
context of one's life. This problem will be
discussed in more detail in a later chapter.

On yet another level, Gemma's intended career
in music and entertainment which was almost
completed as of this writing, points to the
observation that primary migrants who came to Los
Angeles for reasons other than primary group
affiliations, came because no other urban center in
the country was as well known for the particular
specialties they had chosen. For example, this was
true of three of the five individuals who had been
accepted at colleges here. These three had come
explicitly to be trained in aerospace engineering,
this being a field for which Southern California
was the nucleus during the 1950's and 1960's. In
short, they were drawn here by particular needs
that could only be met in a particular place.

It can also be said of those primary migrants
who came here specifically to join kin, fictive
kin, spouse and friends, as well as to enjoy the
pleasant climate, that these particular dual
benefits could not be found elsewhere. Having
someone close to provide a reception in a strange
city is of the utmost importance to Trinidadians,
and also West Indians in general (cf. McLaughlin
1981). The primacy of having primary group
linkages in strange places to which one is
contemplating going may be illustrated by an
encounter I had with a young Trinidadian man whom I
met while on a visit there a year ago. I mentioned
in conversation that I lived in the United States
but was in Trinidad on a visit. He responded by
telling me that he had been wanting to go to the
States on holiday for the longest time, but he
dared not because he knew no one there and
consequently would have no one to put him up or
make his stay enjoyable. In fact, he had never
even ventured as far as Tobago, for the same
reason. For me, this incident captured the essence

of how vital primary social ties can be for migrants, even vacationers.

SECONDARY MIGRATION TO LOS ANGELES

Secondary migrants share in common with primary migrants reasons for coming to Los Angeles such as the appeal of a subtropical climate, acceptance by colleges and recruitment by kin, spouses and friends. The first of these will be discussed here and the remaining reasons will be discussed at a later point. Of the motives for migrating to Los Angeles shared by both primary and secondary migrants, foremost was the Caribbean-like climate here. A sizeable number of participants, 60 percent of both the primary and of the secondary migrants, cited the pleasant weather as the main reason for moving to Los Angeles. This was especially true of those who moved here from the East, who stated in no uncertain terms that the cold of the East had been a terrible shock to them, accustomed as they were to the steaming tropical heat of Trinidad, and that they had come to California to escape the harsh winters. Two women described how the weather brought them to L.A.:

"We found out about California because his mother and sister were living here. Rupert lived here with them but came to Boston and met me there and we got married and started a life and home there. But we didn't like it. The weather wasn't agreeing with me. Couldn't take the winter. . . . . .we packed our belongings and put them in the car and drove across the country and came to California and we've been here ever since."

"I got tired of New York. I figured, well, I'm tired of the weather and the whole thing and I'll come back out to L.A. I like the weather

here, that's what I like about L.A. I don't
know about anything else, but I like the
weather."

However, primary migrants who came directly
from Trinidad also did so because of the weather.
The information dissemination system of migrant
networks had obviously been functioning very
efficiently, as these persons had found out about
the mild climate from kin and/or friends and had
benefitted from it.

At this juncture, the reasons not held in
common by both sets of migrants will be discussed,
as they shed light on some of the differences
between them. One such reason was the appeal of
Los Angeles as a healthier environment for raising
children. Four individuals expressed their concern
that New York was no place for a child to grow up
and had moved here partly because they believed Los
Angeles to be a superior environment. Two of them
said:

"I came here to check the place out. The first
day I came here and see the place, I said, I
ent [aint] going back East. I just fell in
love with it. To me, it was the closest thing
to home. The sunshine. I really like it out
here. Plus, raising a family. To me, this is
a better environment to raise a family."

"I was in New York for six years. New York was
getting to be too much for Bruce [her son].
Well, for me, first of all, and then I thought
of Bruce, he was eighteen months at the time.
We left when I couldn't see him confined to
apartment life or able to go back to Trinidad.
I always had this drive to come to L.A."

One secondary migrant from the East had come to
Los Angeles because of a disappointing experience
with repatriation. This was Roderick Philips,
whose migration history was recounted earlier. He
had emigrated to New York, to change careers, with

the intention of returning to Trinidad with his new
skill.   When he attempted return migration,
however, he met only with frustration.   He then
examined the possibilities in Los Angeles by coming
out here on vacation, a characteristic pattern of
most secondary migrants here.   He liked Los Angeles
because it seemed to combine the virtues of a
climate similar to Trinidad along with some of the
better qualities of New York:

"Living in New York was not my main reason for
going there.   It wasn't a place that I wanted
to live in.   I went there to study.   And when I
was studying, my energy was focussed on that.
Of course, you have to live a little bit, but
once you get your studies out of the way, and
you look for a quality of life, where perhaps
you could look outside (and see trees), you
want to feel a little relaxation at home, you
can't get that from an apartment.   When I walk
down the street here, I see palm trees, I hear
birds singing.   For a Trinidadian who is
accustomed to space, you can understand why
this place is attractive to me.   When I came
here in April and saw the advancement of a big
city and the ease and peace of mind and the
scenery and climatic conditions that I can have
in Trinidad, I said, look, this place provides
these two things. . . I went home and spent the
whole summer primarily to live and not to take
a vacation of three weeks.   I lived there and
saw that I wasn't ready to go back home and
then I came out here."

Another secondary migrant, Felix Coleman,
articulated a unique set of reasons for leaving New
York.   These included his frustration over
stagnation in his career and resentment at being
surrounded by too many West Indian relatives and
friends in New York:

"The more I became ambitious for corporate
leadership, the more I realized that the

influences around me were not directed.   I
couldn't think of one friend I had back then
who had gotten promoted on his job or anything
else.   In fact, Ainsley (his friend) has been
working at Chase Manhattan at the same desk,
doing the same thing for twelve years. He's
still there now. Most of the people in that
department are doing the same thing. I figured
I had two choices. If I stayed, I would lose
face with my friends by ignoring them. If I
went away, I could find someplace without all
these bad influences. That peer influence in
New York among West Indians, Roddy will say the
same thing too, is a force that is worth ten
points in any game. It's a way to really keep
you down.   Because you don't want to make
waves.   You stay in this situation where
everybody is equal in some respects. But the
level of equality is low. If anybody tries to
rise up, they say, what's with him? We not
good enough for him anymore? You must accept a
standard that is substandard. The West Indian
community in New York is probably worse now
than the Puerto Rican community seven years
back. Everybody thinks we all together and we
have these things we can do and be happy.
Moving out to California, I got the same
feeling I got when I was moving from Trinidad
to New York. I felt I was moving one step up.

Part of it was a domestic pressure too.   I
started to resent that I didn't have the
independence in my home life that I needed.
Every weekend, it's either Auntie this or
Auntie that, or cousin this and cousin that.
Probably because I was never part of a big
family setting, I couldn't accept it. I never
felt comfortable.   It was all on Candice's
(wife) side. My weekend was taken over by
somebody else.   Lunch with this person,
Christening here, picnic over there. All these
pressures and the feeling that I couldn't make
headway on my job. I wondered how I could get

away into a setting that is _my_ family setting.
It was a decision to be made by me and my wife,
for the benefit of my kids.   I made the
decision for my family.

One of the reasons I like Los Angeles is
because it doesn't impinge on my lifestyle and
freedom.   I can come home and say, this is what
I'm going to do with my evening.   I couldn't do
that in New York.   There are so many other
people.   Friends, neighbors and others.   Here
in Los Angeles you could live on this street,
drive your car up and down it for seven years,
say hello to your neighbor if you run into him
and still not get involved in the street.   In
New York you have to get involved.   You have to
get involved in the block association,
neighborhood watch, etc.   Or else, you come
home, people are sitting on the steps.   You can
either walk straight through them or you can
hang around and talk with them for a few
minutes. . . You run into people you talk to
for five minutes. . . You see people who take
it for granted that you must spend time with
them because you know them.   Out here in Los
Angeles, distance is what makes. . . you don't
live with each other.   It's hard for somebody
to just drop by.   Nobody in Los Angeles will
attempt to visit you without first contacting
you and making sure you'll be there.   In New
York people turn up at your door.   It's so
close together.   They see your car, they take
it for granted you're home.   It's something I
didn't realize until I came out here.   Mervyn
Dymally says the same thing.   The great thing
about Los Angeles is you can get together with
West Indian friends if you want to, but you
don't have to, if you don't want.   There are a
lot of West Indians living in Los Angeles, but
they not living in any inner city that is
totally West Indian.   If you go to New York
now, you will see exactly what close living has
done to West Indians.   You have this pocket of

people that the city could ignore because they
are all West Indian in there. So now you have
this crime wave that is happening in the West
Indian section of Brooklyn.   The cops say,
those are all foreign people, leave them alone.
And they don't pay attention to them.   They
figure they have this cultural thing together.
If something happens, it happens together."

Felix's narrative was given in graphic detail
because it contains a wealth of insights into West
Indian social life in New York and in Los Angeles,
and suggests essential differences in social
organization between the two cities.   Felix's
account penetrates the dynamics of West Indian
social mobility by revealing how individual
ambition is often thwarted by the tremendously
powerful levelling mechanism of peer pressure,
which maintains the level at the lowest common
denominator.   In Felix's view, the only way of
overcoming this obstacle was escape to a far away
setting.   Felix also complained of a lack of
independence in his home life. There were far too
many kin obligations and his free time seemed to be
dominated either by extended kin or friends or
neighbors, with no time for himself.   Felix felt
constrained by the "closeness" of Afro-Trinidadian
social life in New York where kin and friends are
usually also neighbors.

This impression is corroborated by the findings
of a study of West Indians in New York. Seventy-
five percent (75%) of the sample in this research
admitted to having relatives living in Brooklyn.
Fifty-six percent (56%) had relatives living within
walking distance and eighty-three percent (83%) had
friends living within walking distance (McLaughlin
1981:131).

Dense geographical concentration of this sort
is negative, in Felix's opinion. The scattered
nature of Los Angeles appeals to him because others
cannot just drop in without warning like in New
York. For Felix, then, the move to Los Angeles was
an exercising of his right to freedom of choice:

the option to socialize with other West Indians if desired, and not, if one so chooses. While it must be remembered that Felix was the only one to voice these opinions, all of this provokes the question of how many others in the sample, and in the wider population, perceive the move to Los Angeles as a move to freedom of choice.

For all the reasons just discussed, then, Los Angeles can expect to receive an ever-growing population of Afro-Trinidadians, and West Indians in general, in the coming years. One participant described in his own words, how this is going to happen:

"(West Indians) left friends and family back there. Wrote to them and told them about what opportunities are out here. So you just find a train of migration. Once one arrives, others start to follow. They spread the word around. They tell them it's nice, it's ideal. You don't have to bother with winter. The same day that toilets were frozen in New York, the relative out here was bare-back in the sun. The one in New York start thinking, I have to get out of here and go to L.A. And this has happened over the years, as word of mouth just keeps spreading. So you find more and more West Indians. Pretty soon, you'll find more West Indians here than in New York. They moving out like crazy."

CHAPTER V

MARRIAGE PATTERNS AND KIN-BASED NETWORKS
IN LOS ANGELES

Beginning with the Frazer-Herskovits debate,
black family structure and function in the New
World has been the focus of controversy for several
decades.   In my view, these disputes have been
rooted in the failure to distinguish between four
separate and distinct analytical problems.   These
are marriage, co-residence, kinship and the
organization of domestic activities.   In the Euro-
American cultures from which many researchers
derive, family and household are in practice often
structurally and functionally equivalent.
Consequently, these researchers have mistakenly
equated them when studying cultures in which these
separate domains are not co-terminous.   With the
exception of the work of Carol Stack (1974),
researchers have also failed to address the nature
of the relationships between these distinct
domains.

It is not my intention, in this study of black
immigrants from Trinidad and Tobago, to be drawn
into this debate.   Rather, my purpose in this
chapter is three-fold: 1) to identify patterns of
marriage among participants in the research, 2) to
examine the composition of kin-based networks, and
3) to identify the nature of cooperative domestic
activities both within and across co-residential
units, which ought to reveal the significance of

kin-based relations in the daily lives of Afro-
Trinidadians in Los Angeles.

MARRIAGE PATTERNS

In her study of West Indians in Los Angeles,
Justus (1976) noted that members of her sample
preferred fellow West Indians as mates and that the
ranking of choice ranged from fellow-islanders at
the top, to other West Indians, to Americans of
West Indian ancestry, and lastly, to Americans. To
what extent does this pattern hold true of the
present sample? In Chapter III, I had noted that
eighteen of the thirty sample members were married.
Fifteen of these eighteen married individuals are
married to fellow-Trinidadians. Two of them are
married to black Americans not of West Indian
ancestry, and one to an Afro-Jamaican. Of the
non-married sample members, eight are divorced. To
whom were these individuals married? Three of them
had been married to Afro-Trinidadians, three to
black Americans, one to a white American and one to
an Afro-Jamaican. These marriages lasted from
three to ten years. I observed no association
between country of origin of marital partner and
length of marriage. Of the never-married sample
members, of which there are four, two are members
of consensual unions that have lasted for eight to
nine years with fellow-Trinidadians. One is a
single female with an Afro-Trinidadian boyfriend
and the last is a single male with no lasting
attachments to any members of the opposite sex.
       That fellow-Trinidadians rank highest as
partners in matrimony or amorous liaisons is
obvious. Seventy percent of the sample, twenty-one
participants, are either currently married to, has
been divorced from, or are currently romantically
involved with a fellow-Trinidadian. Thus, as far
as the inclination to choose fellow-islanders as
mates is concerned, my findings concur with those

of Justus (1976). However, it is only in this regard that our findings overlap. For example, she states that at least some of the members of her sample, although she does not specify how many, were already married before migrating. In contrast, not one of the members of this sample were married prior to migration. There was one instance of a participant being romantically linked with her loved one prior to migration and then marrying him later after her arrival. Six others had been slight acquaintances of their spouses before migrating but did not undertake a serious relationship until after they migrated and bumped into each other again.

Apart from these few cases, participants generally met their mates following the move. Participants in this research, therefore, were confronted with acts of choice, more so than those in the Justus study who were already married before the move. Another difference between my findings and those of Justus (1976), is that Americans do not place last in the hierarchy of choices. Both Justus (1976) and I have constructed hierarchies based on behavior. Table 7 shows that 20 percent chose Americans for mates, none of them being of West Indian ancestry. Only 7 percent chose fellow-West Indians, specifically Jamaicans, for mates.

Despite these differences in findings, it is difficult to detect any particular trends from a sample as small as mine. Therefore, I would hesitate to draw any sweeping conclusions from my data. The only finding that is abundantly clear is the unmistakable bias in favor of fellow-Trinidadians. If any pattern of ethnic identification and affiliation is to be inferred from the ethnic membership of mates, then clearly there is an identification as well as affiliation with one's fellow-islanders. These marriage patterns have implications for the lack of assimilation of black immigrants, to be discussed in a later chapter.

THE COMPOSITION OF KIN NETWORKS IN LOS ANGELES

In the pioneering essay in which he laid the
foundations of social network analysis, Mitchell
(1969) identified the need to ascertain the nature
of the links binding individuals to one another.
Among the many possibilities in content are
kinship, friendship, occupation, and neighborhood,
to name only a few. In this section, I shall
stress the kin-based process of interaction.

That kinship was one of the most important
principles of ordering social relations among
Africans in cities was discovered by Epstein (1969)
in his research in a copperbelt town in Central
Africa. The significance of kinship in the urban
social context lies in the capacity of the idiom of
kinship to introduce some measure of stability and
continuity into otherwise mutable social relations
(Epstein 1969:99-101; Jacobson 1971:641).   As
urbanologists have argued, the urban setting is
essentially one of fluidity.   Under these
conditions, expectations of future interaction is
pivotal to the maintenance of relationships
(Jacobson 1971).

According to Jacobson (1971), kinship bonds are
universally recognized as enduring. The injection
of this quality into urban social interaction
favors expectations of continuity. This is not to
say that kin ties may not be broken or that kinship
duties may not be shirked or kinship rights denied.
Nor am I arguing that the degree of kinship
intensity remains forever constant, particularly
during absences.   Rather, the point is that the
banner of kinship has the power to bring together
an assortment of persons who are related through
ties of blood and marriage, in varying degrees of
closeness, and to oblige them to help one another
in most instances (Epstein 1969; Jacobson 1971).
In general, the Afro-Trinidadian immigrants in this
sample honor their responsibilities towards their
kinsmen, although I shall describe exceptions to
this generalization.

What most impressed Epstein (1969) about the social contacts of a participant in his research was the large number and wide range of kin relationsships acknowledged. From this finding, it would seem that the two morphological properties of social networks, size and range, would be the most fruitful to investigate.

The size of kin networks in Los Angeles of the Afro-Trinidadian sample is shown in Table 8. It should be noted that these figures include affines, consanguines, and fictive kin, but only in the intimate zone of social interaction. It can be seen that there is tremendous variation in the size of kin networks in Los Angeles, the two extremes being zero and thirty. At the lower extreme, there are quite a few participants with five or fewer kin in Los Angeles, thirteen individuals to be precise. In the middle ranges, eleven individuals have kin networks in Los Angeles ranging from six to fifteen in number. At the high end of the scale, there are three individuals with relatively large kin networks, twenty-three, twenty-six, and thirty, respectively. The large intimate zones of these latter participants appears to be a function of the presence of numerous siblings.

Apart from these three, the generally small size of kin networks in Los Angeles is not really surprising, given that migrants characteristically leave family members behind. This, coupled with the fact that Los Angeles is a second destination for two-thirds of the sample means that they have left kin in two other locations. As I shall make clear in a later chapter, sample members have kin scattered widely across various parts of the globe.

It is worth pointing out that the variations in kin network size in Los Angeles do not appear to be associated systematically with differences in age, gender, occupation, primary versus secondary migration, or length of residence in Los Angeles. This latter finding is somewhat unexpected as I would have thought that as length of residence increased, so would the number of kin. On the contrary, those who have resided in Los angeles the longest, three individuals who have been here for 24, 26, and 29 years respectively, are the very three participants with no kin in Los Angeles at all.   Long residence and a large kin presence coincided in only one case, that of the participant with the largest kin network of thirty kin, who has been in Los Angeles for 24 years. However, the two individuals with kin networks almost as large, twenty-three and twenty-six kin, have only been in Los angeles for 6 years and 17 years respectively. Thus, no patterned differences are discernible.

While size of social networks is an important structural feature because other structural characteristics are calculated as proportions of the total number of links, size alone gives limited information about the nature of these links.   More revealing of the content of kinship links is the range of kin relationships or the composition of kin networks.   By far the most common type of kin network is the two-generational one of which there are three variants.   The main differences between these variants of two-generational networks lie in the presence or absence of lateral kin, for example, siblings and cousins, as well as the presence or absence of spouses of lateral kin and kin of one's spouse, plus the children of the above.   In short, while two-generational kin networks may be shallow, they exhibit great breadth.   Two-generational networks also point to the importance of spouses and affinal kin relationships.

Although fewer sample members belong to three-generational kin networks than to two-generational ones, the fact that nine participants, 30 percent of the sample, belong to kin networks of such depth is quite striking. With regards to fictive kin, it should be mentioned that although only one participant had kin that fell strictly into the category of fictive, four others acknowledged the presence of fictive kin in addition to real kin. Furthermore, the presence of large numbers of lateral kin and spouses of lateral kin, as well as kin of spouses in three-generational networks,

underscores of importance of affinal relationships.
Even more impressive than three-generational
networks are the four-generational networks of two
sample members, in terms of depth. As with size,
differences in the range of kin relationships do
not appear to coincide with variations in age,
gender, socio-economic status, neighborhood, length
of residence, or other factors.

THE CONTENT OF KIN INTERACTION IN LOS ANGELES

So far, only the structure of kin relations in
Los Angeles has been discussed, not the substance
of kin interaction. In this section, I examine the
content of interaction of Afro-Trinidadian kin
networks in Los Angeles, including features such as
multiplexity, transactional content, intensity,
frequency, duration, and whether kin lie in the
intimate, effective, or extended zones of kin
relations. To begin with, multiplexity is a
measure of the degree to which a network link
involves more than one social role. For example,
two individuals may be linked simultaneously as
kinsman and colleagues or as kinsman and neighbor,
or possibly all three. Multiplexity seems to be
quite scarce in the Afro-Trinidadian sample. Only
seven individuals, 23 percent, had overlap of
content. Two participants were business partners
with a sibling in Los Angeles. Three individuals
owned property in common with siblings or cousins
in Los Angeles. Two members of the sample had
similar occupations as another kinsman. Thus,
there is slight overlap of the roles of kinsman and
colleague.
   In my view, the low incidence of concurrence
between kinship and occupation among Afro-
Trinidadians is due to the tremendous occupational
diversity of West Indians in general. Unlike other
immigrant groups in the history of U.S. immigration
who concentrated in particular occupational niches,

Afro-Trinidadians, and other West Indians as well, are highly diversified in terms of occupation. McLaughlin (1981) found similar occupational diversity in her sample in New York. This contrasts, for instance, with the concentration of Poles in the steel industry of eastern cities earlier in the century, and with the concentration of Mexicans in farm labor today. Predictably, the coincidence of kinship and occupation among West Indians would be low under these conditions of variations in skills.

Concurrence of kin and neighbor roles is also conspicuously absent in the Afro-Trinidadian sample in Los Angeles. This situation is the converse of that of West Indian immigrants in New York who, according to McLaughlin (1981), were frequently both kinsmen and neighbors. In fact, 56 percent of the New York sample had relatives living within walking distance. In Los Angeles, Afro-Trinidadians are separated from one another by considerable distances, generally speaking, due to the dispersed nature of Los Angeles geography. Within the sample, there are only two exceptions to this rule. One exception is a three-generational kin network whose members live within a mile or two of each other. Although the Prices do not fit my definition of neighbors, they live reasonably close together by Los Angeles standards. In fact, this fifteen-member kin network had been actual neighbors a year or two prior to the beginning of my research, when they occupied three contiguous apartments in the same building. Because the kin network included six children, they were forced to move when the landlord changed his renting policy to exclude children. As a result, they bought homes within a two-mile radius of each other.

There is another example of nearby kin: the Sinclairs, a four-generational kin network in which ego, spouse, and two children reside in one household, and ego's mother and grandmother live together in a home only a few blocks away. Both of these cases will be discussed in greater detail. None of the other participants have kin living nearby except for those who are already part of the household as houseguests.

Although there is very little overlap of kinship roles with neighbor roles or kinship with occupational roles, there is some overlap of kinship and friendship. Indeed, close friendships are sometimes indistinguishable from kinship relations in terms of rights and duties. When kinship and friendship overlap in any one link, it makes that tie exceptionally binding. Only a small percentage of links may be characterized in this way. There is some overlap of the roles of friend and work associate, although not very common. Concurrence of kin and work associate roles is virtually absent. In sum, multiplexity does not appear to be an outstanding attribute of the social relationships of the sample members, generally speaking.

THE IMPORTANCE OF KINSHIP IN DAILY LIFE IN L.A.

Perhaps the most illuminating of all the properties of interaction is transactional content or the nature of material and non-material elements exchanged. This is because the nature of transactions discloses not only the quality of social interaction, but its significance compared with other social relations. Since exchange is usually based on reciprocity, the content of reciprocity provides clues as to what benefits might accrue from such interaction (Boissevain 1974:33). There appear to be no gender differences in transactional content.

Owning property in common is one type of transaction engaged in by only one of the sample members, together with three of his siblings in Los Angeles. This individual is Colin Dexter, whose remarkably successful real estate ventures were described in Chapter IV. Colin also owns property in common in Miami with his mother who lives there and is involved in real estate deals with close Trinidadian friends in Los Angeles. As he himself put it, "Wheelin' an' dealin' man! You got to wheel and deal to make money in this country." Two other participants, a brother and sister, were involved as business partners in a small restaurant in Los Angeles. Their foray into the business world was both brief and unsuccessful as their restaurant went bankrupt after 6 months, partly due to under-capitalization and partly as a result of poor choice of location. Based on the small proportion of the sample engaged in small businesses, it does not seem as though Afro-Trinidadians have a great propensity for enterprise, as claimed by Light (1972) in his book on ethnic enterprise.[2] More participants are involved in the giving and receiving of information relating to the job market, locating housing, and getting legal advice, than in enterprise.

Two types of kin transaction that appear to be salient for a large proportion of the sample are transportation and child care services. As testimony to their importance, a total of twenty-five participants, or 83 percent of the sample, are engaged in these two activities. Not surprisingly, these two domains are most important to those with young children or elderly kin or both. Various sample members have come up with different solutions to their child care problems. One participant, Heather Johnson, has invited her husband's younger sister from the U.S. Virgin Islands to live with her and her husband in Los Angeles in order to take care of their 8-year-old daughter, Tamara. This solution has only been in effect for just under a year. Before that, her two older sons from a previous marriage used to mind Tamara when they still lived at home and were going to school. Heather was forced to seek another solution when the two elder boys joined the U.S. military and moved far away after finishing high school. As far as the other problem of school transportation for Tamara, Heather and her husband, Neil, share the burden almost equally.

A different arrangement had been worked out by the Prices, the three-generational kin network mentioned previously. They lived within a couple of miles of each other and devised a system of child-care and transportion for the six children included in the network. Originally, the network consisted of fifteen members and occupied four different households. One household contained Mrs. Price, a woman in her fifties, her daughter Shelley, son-in-law Stanley and twin grand-daughters Stacey and Tiffany. In a second household lived another daughter, Denise, another son-in-law, Geoffrey, and another grand-daughter, Robin. In a third household lived a third daughter, Marilyn, a third son-in-law, Roland, and a third grand-daughter, Gillian. However, Marilyn and Roland divorced a year ago, and Roland has gone back to New York to live with his parents. Denise and Geoffrey have also divorced, but Geoffrey has remained in Los Angeles. A fourth household contained a son, Terence, his wife, Janet, and their two children, Adam and Angela, as well as Janet's brother Derek. In the initial stages of my research, the Prices had come to a mutual agreement whereby Mrs. Price would mind all six children between the time school let out and the time the children's parents got home from work. With respect to transportation to and from school, the parents of the children took turns in rotation. Occasionally, when an emergency arose, Derek, Janet Price's brother, would pitch in and provide transportation as well as baby sit.

The plan fell apart for several reasons. First of all, a year after my research began, Mrs. Price left Los Angeles and went back to New York to seek medical care from a Trinidadian doctor because she does not trust the American doctors in Los Angeles she has consulted. Hence, Mrs. Price was no longer available as the babysitter for the children. Second, a year ago, a family quarrel broke out over the payment of the mortgage for the house in which Mrs. Price used to live, causing the Price siblings to take sides. At the same time, Marilyn and

Denise divorced their husbands, behavior that was
disapproved of by their mother and siblings. The
combination of the family dispute and the divorces
have resulted in ostracism for Marilyn and Denise
who are shunned by their siblings, Terence and
Shelley, and their respective spouses. Strangely
enough, all six grand-children are still on good
terms, and Geoffrey, Denise's ex-husband, is still
on very friendly terms with his former siblings-in-
law. The culmination of all these developments has
been that the children have been placed in extended
day care centers when not in school. Terence and
Janet and Shelley and Stanley still rotate the
transportation of the children to and from school
and day care.

The Sinclairs, the four-generational kin
network also described earlier, have arrived at a
strategy quite similar to the original plan of the
Prices. The Sinclair network also spans several
households. Rupert and his wife, Maureen, and
their two daughters, Michelle and Jennifer, live in
one household in Inglewood. A couple of blocks
away live Rupert's mother, Enid, and grandmother
Melda. Enid and Melda take care of Michelle and
Jennifer when they are out of school and Rupert and
Maureen are not yet home from work. Rupert's
sister, Darlene, lives quite far away in the San
Fernando Valley. Maureen's three younger
brothers, Neville, Dudley, and Walter, live in
Pasadena, also quite far away. Occasionally, when
the two older women are not available, Rupert's
sister or one or more of Maureen's brothers will
look after the girls. Rupert and Maureen transport
not only their daughters to and from school, but
also Rupert's 93-year-old grandmother to church and
various other places. From time to time, Maureen's
mother, who lives in Trinidad and Tobago, comes to
stay as a houseguest for about a year or so and
helps Maureen with the children and housework.

Apart from the kin networks just described,
there are others in the sample in a similar
predicament of having young children and having to
find a means to care for them while adults are at

work. As it turns out, most of the others also depend on siblings, siblings' spouses, or spouses' siblings for this service. A few rely on cousin(s), their spouse(s), or spouse's cousin(s) for the same. The few without access to any of the above resources, three participants only, have no choice but to turn to individual babysitters who are trustworthy or to day care centers. The wife of the multi-millionaire, Colin Dexter, is the only female who is strictly a housewife and stays home with the children when they are out of school. However, even if Colin's wife were not available, Colin would have no difficulty finding help in looking after his children because Colin has numerous siblings, siblings' spouses, cousins, and cousins' spouses in Los Angeles, his kin network in Los Angeles being the one with thirty members. At least one of them should be able to help mind his children. These findings underscore yet again the instrumental importance of broad local kin relationships, including collaterals and affines.

By far the most common form of kin transaction in Los Angeles is sharing one's home with various types of kin, both sharing it as a host and as a houseguest. As one would expect, sharing with spouse and children occurs most often. Five childless individuals share with only their spouses. Two spouseless individuals share with only their child. A handful share their home with their sibling(s) and another handful with spouse's kin, again reinforcing the importance of siblings and spouse's kin. One shared with a cousin, another with a grandnephew, and a third with fictive kin. Although these categories have been separated out for analytical purposes, there is some overlap of categories. For example, several participants share their homes with spouse and children, as well as with siblings and spouse's kin.

Being a houseguest of one's kin is also fairly common, as was the case for six of the participants. It is especially necessary for houseguests to contribute at least grocery money

and perhaps rent money, as well as to help toward
the viability of the household.   Relatives like
cousins, siblings, nephews, spouse's kin, and
fictive kin are obliged to donate something to the
household in which they live, whether it be in the
form of money, material goods, or some type of
service, such as housework.   There is apparently an
optimal length of time spent living with a relative
before one wears out one's welcome.   As one
participant, Roderick Philips, put it:

> This is another thing that is characteristic of
> new arrivals here. You start off staying by a
> person who encourages you to stay.   I was
> staying by my cousin. . .You could stay by a
> relative or a friend for just about six months
> without feeling that you are encroaching on
> their lives.

Although Roderick specified a threshold of six
months, four of the houseguests in the sample
stayed only for about two months. However, two of
the six stayed for over two years with siblings.
The extenuating circumstances in both cases were
that neither individual was in a position to find
another living arrangement since they were both
unemployed.
Lest I give the impression that Afro-
Trinidadians maintain kinship ties for strictly
instrumental reasons, I shall turn to interaction
of sociability for its own sake. It is traditional
for Afro-Trinidadians to have large family
gatherings for special meals on special occasions,
such as Christmas and other major holidays in their
homeland.   They have not abandoned the custom
since coming to America and continue to do so on
Christmas, July 4th, and other holidays.   At a
glance, this may not appear very different from
Euro-American holiday behavior.   The major
difference lies in the type of food. No turkeys or
ham, only traditional Trinidadian food, such as
callaloo and crab, souse, and other savory dishes.
Whereas everyday meals for Afro-Trinidadians

usually include only household members, holiday
meals incorporate the entire kin network of all
generations, as well as close family friends.

Janet Price recounted a traditional Christmas
meal in New York and how Christmas celebrations had
changed since moving to Los Angeles:

> For Christmas [in New York], Terence's mum and
> they used to have a big cook out and stuff, and
> it used to be real nice. . His family usually
> gets together and stuff and have a real big
> cook out. About 24 of them or even more. His
> aunts and them. Everybody gets together. We
> still have it here in California, but it isn't
> as big as back East.

Thus even if the entire kin network does not
interact at any other time, which is unlikely, at
least they do so on special occasions for holiday
banquets. Everyone in the gathering pools food,
drink, and supplies, as well as labor for cooking
and cleaning. Hosting is done by the unit with
facilities large enough to accommodate everyone.

Among West Indians in general, Trinidadians
have a reputation for having a "carnival
mentality," in other words, their main interest in
life lies in dancing, partying, and things
frivolous. While this is certainly an
exaggeration, it is undeniable that Trinidadians
love to "fete," as the Trinidadian expression goes.
Indeed, rumor has it that during the 1970 Black
Power Revolt in Trinidad and Tobago, the late Prime
Minister, Eric Williams, said: "Not to worry.
Just give dem a little `fete', a little `pan-on-de-
road' [steelband music] and dey will quiet down."
Whether or not Trinidadians like to "fete" more
than other West Indians is difficult for me to
judge on a systematic basis since this was not a
comparative study of the various West Indian groups
in Los Angeles. My impression is that Afro-
Trinidadians are more exceptionally fond of
partying than other West Indians.

At this point, I must mention that the subject under discussion is house dancing parties or private gatherings in someone's home, restricting guests to personal friends, kin, and friends of friends. This is in contrast to dances held at a public venue, open to the public, for which admission is charged. House parties are hosted by only half the sample members approximately, and then only about every three to four months. Unlike family banquets, house parties are not limited to just kin, although kin are certainly invited, especially those of approximately equal age. Guests at house parties are selected from different fields of interaction: kin, friends, co-workers, possibly neighbors, fellow sportsmen, friends of friends, and so forth.

In a city, such as Los Angeles, whose basic physical characteristic is geographical dispersion, telephone conversations between those separated by distances would logically assume at least equal, if not greater, significance than face-to-face interaction. In Los Angeles, the telephone is vital to the viability of kin networks. Telephone conversations between kinsmen in Los Angeles generally consist of an exchange of general information, an update on what is happening in their daily lives and the lives of other family members (both general and specific), unusual events, as well as gossip, in a judgmental and non-judgmental sense. News from home is quickly shared with kinsmen, via the telephone, to keep each other abreast of current events in Trinidad and Tobago. It might seem strange, then, that not all of the sample members participate in this form of interaction. This is partly due to the fact that three individuals have no kin in Los Angeles with whom to converse. But, in addition, five other participants have no need to have regular telephone interaction with kin in Los Angeles because they live within the same household as these kin and engage in ongoing, face-to-face interaction on a daily basis. Thus, only twenty-

two individuals, or 73 percent of the sample,
practice this type of kin transaction.

Frequency is an important measure of
interaction. With respect to telephone
conversations between kin in Los Angeles occupying
separate households, frequency depends on whether
the interacting dyads are located in either the
intimate, effective, or extended zones of social
relations. For the most part, relatives in Los
Angeles of the Afro-Trinidadian sample tend to
occupy positions mostly in the intimate or
effective zone. Generally speaking, those who
share a household comprise a portion of, but do not
exhaust, the limits of the intimate zone. Kin
residing in different households in Los Angeles may
nevertheless be included in the intimate zone by
being on the closest of terms. For example, in the
Price and Sinclair networks described above, face-
to-face and telephone interaction transcends
household boundaries and occurs daily, sometimes
several times in a day. Nor is the intimate zone
confined by geographical boundaries. The intimate
zone may include close kin in other North American
cities, close kin in the West Indies, or even close
friends in various places. The intimate zone is
here defined as comprising those relationships that
bear the greatest emotional intensity.

The frequency of telephone conversations
between kin in the intimate zone in Los Angeles
varies from several times daily, just described, to
daily, to three times a week, to as infrequently as
once every two weeks. Ten participants, one-third
of the sample, interact with kin on the telephone
daily. Five of them do so three times a week, and
seven of them only do so every other week. The
rest either interact on a face-to-face basis or
have no kin here. Of course, these are average
frequencies which change depending on
circumstances. For example, in a crisis, frequency
may increase.

In their homeland, it is customary for
Trinidadians of all races to drop by and "lime."
But "liming" implies more than standing around on

street corners, although that is also done.
"Liming" is spending time relaxing with one's
fellows, kin, friends, or acquaintances, "ole
talking" (chatting in a leisurely manner) and often
drinking. It can be done out on the streets or
indoors. The main point is being unhurried and
unconstrained by time. In other words, the typical
Trinidadian pattern of visiting relatives and
friends, on a regular basis, is to do so
spontaneously and without appointment.
Apparently, Trinidadians in New York have not
abandoned this custom, according to the testimony
of Felix Coleman. To what extent has it continued
in Los Angeles? Several participants lamented that
it is dying out or may even be extinct already.
Although the preferred mode of interaction is
"dropping by," the Los Angeles metropolitan
setting is not conducive to this. More and more,
Trinidadians in Los Angeles are learning to accept
pre-arranged visits as a way of life. This is
Gemma Jones complaint:

> I think that's the main thing I don't like
> about life in the States. Growing up at home,
> you get so close to people, and you have a lot
> of family and friends all around. And you
> could drop in anytime. But here you can't do
> that. If you don't call first, you're in
> trouble. It's a different style, but I'm
> adapting to it. I find that everybody here is
> so wrapped up in their own lives, including
> Trinidadians who are here. They don't drop in
> anymore. They're just like the Americans.
> When they get together, it's always a planned
> thing, and arrangements have to be made ahead
> of time. None of this dropping by and liming
> for a while like in Trinidad. People in
> Trinidad have to work and have children too,
> but somehow they manage to drop in and lime.

Kenneth Simpson also bemoaned the disappearance of "dropping by and liming" and told how hard he was trying to keep up the custom:

There are quite a few West Indians here, but I don't think we are as close as we should be. Los Angeles is so large and scattered. And you know Trinidadians, we grew up with an inherent habit of dropping by and not phoning or making appointments. And you can't do that here. I have some friends who live in Baldwin Hills, and I prefer to drop by all the way from the Valley instead of calling to see if they're home. . .I don't want to give up the habit. That's one of the things I miss here, people just dropping by and liming a little bit. Trinidadians love to ole-talk. I mean it's part of our culture!

Despite these complaints, however, "dropping by and liming" does not appear to be dead and buried. I have personally observed Trinidadians dropping by while I was in several participant's homes. And, Colin Dexter has told me that he "love to ole-talk wid his 'pardners' too bad and lime wid de fellas and a bottle of Old Oak or Vat 19 (Trinidadian rums)." They talk about Reagan, Chambers (current Prime Minister of Trinidad), or what someone had to say who just came back from Trinidad and Tobago. That's how he keeps up with what is going on around him. With the exception of Kenneth Simpson, it seems as though those who practice "dropping by and liming" live relatively close to one another.

The frequency of visiting again depends on whether the interacting dyad is located in the intimate or effective zone. Kin located in the intimate zone in Los Angeles visit each other as often as daily, as do four of the participants. One or two see each other five times per week. A half dozen visit three times per week, and only one or two do so only once per week. In the effective zone, a handful visit each other every other week or so, and another handful only visit about once a month. Many of these visits to relatives take the form of "dropping and liming," although not always.

Durability of network links is a characteristic that deserves more elaboration when applied to contexts of friendship, as opposed to those of kinship, although durability of kin relationships can vary according to whether they are consanguineal or affinal. Consanguineal relationships are presumed to last the lifetime of an individual, starting at birth and ending at death. Thus, the duration of blood ties, in principle, coincides with the age of an individual. In practice, of course, blood ties sometimes rupture, as in the case of the Prices, but are not necessarily permanently broken. For instance, the Prices are slowly healing their breach. On the other hand, affinal relationships are generally of shorter duration since they do not begin until marriage, when an individual is already an adult. In addition, affinal relationships are by nature more brittle than blood ties, which is to say, separation and divorce are comparatively easier than estrangement from consanguineal relatives. Rupturing of nuptial agreements tend to be more permanent, although amicable relations can continue after divorces. Duration of affinal ties in the sample ranged from 5 years to 28 years, depending on the age of the individual.

While it is important to consider the intensity of network links between individuals, even Mitchell (1969) concedes that efforts to quantify this feature have been unsuccessful. Thus, it is left up to the researcher to evaluate the emotional value invested in a particular relationship, which is often a highly subjective judgment. It seems to me that intensity of feeling in a relationship, whether in the context of kinship or of friendship, is a function of whether or not the link is located in the intimate zone of social relations. As I shall demonstrate in a subsequent chapter, the intimate zone of each sample member is not confined by geography, but extends to other cities of North America, the West Indies, and other parts of the world.   Nor is it restricted to kinsmen; it also extends to friends acquired in various contexts.   However, intimate and trustworthy local kinsmen are indispensable to the daily functioning of immigrants in a new land. They play a pivotal role in the adaptation process by preserving cultural traditions and at the same time furnishing a firm footing from which to launch newly acquired behavior patterns.

CHAPTER VI

TRANSCONTINENTAL AND TRANSNATIONAL
KIN-BASED NETWORKS

Although kin ties may be broken, and have been
by participants in the research (as I have
described above), generally speaking, kinship bonds
are more enduring than other primary relationships.
That this is so is evidenced by the fact that
sample members maintain ties with kin in other
cities of North America, such as New York; parts of
New Jersey; Washington, D.C.; Hartford,
Connecticut; New Haven, Connecticut; Miami;
Houston; San Francisco; Montreal; Toronto; Calgary;
and Vancouver.

TRANSCONTINENTAL KIN NETWORKS IN NORTH AMERICA

The size of kin networks in the cities
mentioned above is shown in Table 8. The total
number of kin in these North American cities
combined is approximately equal to those in Los
Angeles, but their distribution among participants
is different from those in Los Angeles. It should
be remembered that these figures include only the
intimate zone of social relations. The majority of
sample members have close relatives, such as
parents, siblings, siblings' spouses, and siblings'

105

children, in other cities of North America. A few
have first and more distant cousins with whom they
are on close terms.   One or two are on intimate
terms with uncles, aunts, and cousins, and one or
two are on such terms with former spouses and
children.

Almost half of the sample have links with two
generations of kin, mostly consisting of the
sibling generation and the generation of their
siblings' children, or else, cousins and their
children.   Twenty percent of the sample belong to
three-generational kin networks in other cities,
comprised of the parental, sibling, and siblings'
children generations.   The nature of these kin
relationships and their placement in the intimate
zone of social relations, despite wide dispersion
across the North American continent, implies
intensity of interaction that transcends
geographical boundaries, although not necessarily
of a frequent or face-to-face nature.

A comparison of kin networks in Los Angeles
with those in other cities of North America shows
that whereas two-generational networks in Los
Angeles tend to be built around spouse, children
and siblings, their spouses and children, in other
cities of North America there tend to be far more
parents and their spouses, siblings and their
spouses and children, cousins, as well as uncles
and aunts and their respective spouses.   Three-
generational networks in other cities of North
America include more first cousins and parents than
those in Los Angeles. Finally, there are two four-
generational networks in Los Angeles but none
elsewhere.

THE CONTENT OF TRANSCONTINENTAL KIN NETWORKS

There is much interaction of an extensive
nature, back and forth across the North American
continent, as shown in Table 9.   It should be

pointed out that Table 9 includes only the intimate zone of interaction.

The exchange of letters is one form of interaction. Many participants told me bluntly that they detested letter writing and simply refused to do it. The truth of this can be seen in the fact that only eleven individuals exchange letters with kin in other regions of North America, and these only do so on a monthly basis or even less frequently (see Table 9). Most prefer to keep in touch with kin by telephone, even though it is far more expensive and could mean less frequent communication as a result.

Interestingly enough, however, one of the participants, Yvette Harris, has a cousin in New Haven, Connecticut who is sufficiently imbued with a sense of kinship and family pride to have constructed a genealogy of the Harris "clan," tracing it back to St. Lucia. She has also been inspired enough to write a family newsletter regularly which she distributes annually to every branch of the Harris family scattered across the globe. The newsletter tells about births, deaths, marriages, and other eventful things that have happened to the Harrises; for example, when Yvette gave birth to her little boy, it was written about in the newsletter. Six years ago, this cousin organized a family reunion of the Harrises that took place in Trinidad. A plane had to be chartered to transport the hundreds of Harrises who attended.

While letter writing may not be very popular among members of the sample, post-industrial electronic marvels like the long distance telephone certainly are. Table 9 shows that all of the twenty-four participants with kin in North America contact them by telephone with considerable frequency. Ten of them do so once a week or even more often. Another nine do so at least once a month or more often and only five telephone less often than once a month. In talking with me about the frequency of long distance telephone conversations, Monica Gonzalez confided how intense kin relationships can be even across thousands of miles:

> I keep in touch with my family in New York. I talk to my mother about every other day or so. And Ralph (her husband) and his sister (who lives in New York) are very close. They talk to each other all the time. Half a month's salary goes to paying the long distance phone bill. I think we could have had a house (by now) if it wasn't for these phone bills.

If letter writing between cities in North America seems uncommon, remittances are even more so. Only two participants send remittances to kin in other cities. One of them is Heather Johnson, the individual described earlier who had invited her sister-in-law from the U.S. Virgin Islands to live with her and her husband so that her sister-in-law could take care of her 8-year-old daughter, Tamara. Heather sends remittances to her mother who now lives in New York because her mother cared for her two sons who stayed in Trinidad for the first 5 years after Heather had migrated from Trinidad and Tobago to the United States. Even though her two sons from her first marriage are now fully grown and no longer even live at home, Heather acknowledges her gratitude to her mother by sending her money regularly for accepting full responsibility for keeping the two boys between the ages of 2 and 8 years, during a period of Heather's life when she could not have the boys with her in the early stages of migration.

The other participant who sends remittances is Colin Dexter, the multi-millionaire. He regularly sends money to his mother who lives in Miami. He also owns property in Miami in common with his mother. As a result, he visits Miami regularly, about once a month, and stays with his mother as her houseguest, to visit with her as well as check on his property. He also calls her long distance from Los Angeles every other week.

Only two sample members send child support to former mates for their children from other marriages or relationships. Neil Johnson, now Heather's husband, has several children other than Tamara, his 8-year-old daughter from his marriage to Heather. He has a 16-year-old daughter, from a teenage romance in Trinidad, who lives with her mother in Toronto. He also has a child from another relationship who lives in the South with the child's mother. He has two sons from a previous marriage who live with their mother in New York. He has always kept in touch with his 16-year-old daughter in Toronto and has sent child support regularly. In fact, she spent a summer in Los Angeles two years ago as Neil and Heather's houseguest.

However, he has not been on good terms with his ex-wife in New York until recently, nor with his child in the South and the mother of this child, so he did not send support to either of them on a regular basis. Although he would like to be a more dutiful father, he has suffered financial hardships for the past several years since the recession began. As a skilled craftsman, he has only been employed intermittently over the past 3 years. He is therefore in no position to provide more support for his children in other cities. Another participant sends money once a month to New York to the mother of his son, born of a romance that ended long ago. Except for regular remittances and letters, he does not maintain a relationship with her.

Sending children to live with relatives in other cities of North America is less common than sending them to live in the West Indies or leaving them there. In fact, only four participants have done so. The situation of one of the four, Yvette Harris, is detailed here. Yvette is on very close terms with one of her sisters who lives in New York with her husband and two children. Yvette chats on the phone with her sister about twice a week. Last summer Yvette was in a terrible bind and had no choice but to send her 8-year-old son, Bruce, to

live with her sister for the duration of the
summer.   Yvette had started a business in Los
Angeles in partnership with one of her brothers.
Since both Yvette and her brother had to tend to
the store from morning till night and were seldom
home, Bruce was being neglected tremendously.   He
was either left alone at home or taken to the store
to spend all day and evening there.   Neither
arrangement was satisfactory.   Bruce's father, from
whom Yvette is divorced, had moved out of town and
was unable to share in the care of Bruce.   In
desperation, Yvette sent Bruce to live with her
sister in New York until a better solution could be
worked out.   Bruce returned to Los Angeles at the
end of the summer.   In exchange, Yvette's sister in
New York sent both her children to Los Angeles for
Yvette to mind during the Summer Olympics of 1984.
"Child-fostering" will be discussed in greater
detail below.

THE WEST INDIAN SOCIAL WORLD IN NEW YORK COMPARED
WITH LOS ANGELES

     In the course of my research, several
participants painted a portrait for me of the
social world of West Indians in New York.   In their
perceptions, there are many contrasts in social
life between New York and Los Angeles.   In Chapter
IV, Felix Coleman already described the intensity
and frequency of kin interactions when he and his
wife lived in New York.   Every weekend there was
some sort of social gathering with uncles, aunts,
and cousins, either for lunches, picnics, or more
formal occasions, such as christenings.   Besides
social closeness, Felix also described dense
geographical concentration of kin in New York:

     If you buy a house, they want you to buy one
     next door or one that is big enough so it can
     be shared.

In fact, when they lived in New York, he and his wife lived in an apartment in a four-plex owned by his wife's parents who lived in the same building, as did his wife's sisters and brothers, single and married.

But, whereas Felix Coleman found this situation oppressive, Monica and Ralph Gonzalez do not. Indeed, having moved to Los Angeles from New York 13 years ago, they had contemplated moving back to New York about 7 years ago.   This was because Monica's parents had at that time bought a house across the street from the home owned by Monica's sister in eager anticipation of Monica and Ralph's return and in expectation of their sharing this house, as "a family thing" in Monica's words.   The Gonzalezes in Los Angeles ended up not returning to New York because of what they considered social degeneration of Brooklyn.   But had they done so, they would have lived in the sort of domestic units observed by McLaughlin (1981) in her study of West Indians in New York: adult children often continue to live with their parents whether single or married, in the same building, if not in the same apartment.

Apart from density in kin relationships, in both a geographical and social sense, friendships in New York City are also distinctive. Monica and Ralph Gonzalez revealed the nature of the social world of Afro-Trinidadians in New York and their relations with other West Indian groups:

In New York, they (West Indians) tend to stay within their own island groups.   Trinidadians stick together, Jamaicans the same and the Haitians the same.   Everybody in their own clan.   Sometimes Jamaicans have hang-ups (conflicts) with Trinidadians and so on.   It's freer now than before.   I don't know that much about out here.   I see the Jamaicans and I hear about them, but I don't have any for friends, so I don't run into many of them. . .To me, it follows the same patterns.   The few friends we have out here are Trinidadians.

Gemma Jones, who has not lived in New York but has a best friend who lived there for a while, relates a similar observation:

You know there's something of a little Trinidad up there in New York. My best friend was telling me how Trinidadians like to keep to themselves and "lime" with themselves and not really go anywhere and find out about their new environment.

Roderick Philips, a secondary migrant from New York, describes social relations among Trinidadians in New York and why he moved here:

Brooklyn is in many respects more Trinidadian than Trinidad. Brooklyn is so much like the Trinidad that I know, for the simple reason that you have the food, the music, and a lot of my friends from back home. . .

One of the reasons I left Brooklyn was my circle of friends was becoming too large. They were taking up all my time, and I didn't have time for other pursuits. I like to write. Short stories. I was doing too much socializing. My house was always open. People would come over. I like to entertain. . People would call me up in the night and come across. . .So, I came here (to Los Angeles) to cut down on the socializing. But I like to know it's there. I wouldn't have come out here unless I knew there was a West Indian community here. I must have that reference group. I mightn't mix with them as often as I did back home or in Brooklyn, but. . .

The West Indian social world in New York, then, may be characterized as dense in kin relationships, dense in friendships with "home-fellows," as well as filled with inter-island rivalries. But, the essence of the West Indian way of life in New York as distilled by many participants seems to be "partying." A major complaint of many participants was that social life in Los Angeles was "dead" compared to New York. Partying seems to be a fundamental component of the New York scene, as one participant's husband told me:

In Brooklyn, you could go to a party any time you want. Somewhere there's a party all the time. With all the West Indians in Brooklyn, you have a lot of parties to choose from. Every Saturday, there's a party here and everywhere.

Felix Coleman described the same phenomenon:

In New York, West Indians have parties every weekend. Basement or house parties. Some people try to make a little money by charging $2 or so. There's partying going on all the time.

The husband of another participant had this to say about social life in New York:

"Fetes" have always been a way of life for me. I'm a party type of guy. In fact, in New York, we used to give parties to the point where I was thinking seriously of quitting my job. I used to make good money throwing parties. New York is a partying place. It's a way of life. Everybody goes out to party in New York. . . Los Angeles is definitely more of a police-state than New York. . .For instance, if you give a party out here and the neighbors complain, the cops come and close down the party in a minute. . .Because you find that people out here do not have that partying spirit as they do back East. When the same people come out here, they start to follow a different rhythm, for some reason.

In what ways, then, does social life in New York contrast with social life in Los Angeles for

Afro-Trinidadians? The obvious differences are the mild climate and the slower and more relaxed pace of life in Los Angeles compared with the hustle and bustle of New York. Some participants describe Los Angeles as "quiet," others as "sedentary," and yet others as "dead." A crucial difference from the perspective of social relations is the dissimilar visiting patterns. Monica Gonzalez described the contrast in this way:

> New York is more compact. West Indian people are concentrated in one or two areas. But in Los Angeles, they live so far away and so far apart that visiting them becomes a major production that you can only do on special days like holidays for a treat. In New York, you would get up on a Sunday and just drop by.

In other words, there are perceptions of significant contrasts in the density of kin networks, as well as friendship networks, between the two cities. There seems to be only one domain in which social life in Los Angeles is not dramatically different from that in New York, and this domain is ethnic chauvinism or "clannishness," as Ralph Gonzalez called it:

> They are clannish out here too. The most is Belizeans. They stay together and have their clubs and their social activities. You find the same thing with Trinidadians, although you find that at large functions, like if they have Sparrow here, you'll find more of a mix of different West Indians. . .Too, there are quite a few Panamanians out here. I went to a couple of their boat rides. You don't really see them. That's the problem here (in Los Angeles) because they're all so spread out. It's only when you go to a function and see them all together that you realize how many are here. . In terms of socializing, they stick together within their own group.

It would appear that Afro-Trinidadians both in Los Angeles and in New York prefer to remain encapsulated within a social world filled with others just like themselves. Only time will tell if life in Los Angeles will erode this preference.

TRANSNATIONAL KIN NETWORKS IN THE WEST INDIES

As evidence of the widely scattered nature of Afro-Trinidadian kin networks, one-third of the sample, ten individuals, have relatives remaining not only in Trinidad and Tobago, but other Caribbean countries, such as Jamaica, Barbados, St. Vincent, and the U.S. Virgin Islands. These participants in the research are either descendents of migrants from these territories to Trinidad and Tobago, or the converse, or are married to persons with kin there. The rest of the sample, without exception, have kin remaining only in Trinidad and Tobago. The size of kin networks in the West Indies is similar to that of Los Angeles, as shown in Table 8. It will be recalled that these figures include consanguines, affines, and fictive kin. It is noteworthy that while there were three participants without any kin in Los Angeles, there is not a single participant without kin in the West Indies. But, a comparison of size of kin networks in Los Angeles with that in the West Indies reveals a different distribution. At the lowest end of the spectrum in the West Indies, the smallest number of kin was one, and at the opposite extreme, the largest number of kin was 25. In between, most sample members have between eleven and fifteen kin remaining in the West Indies. Considering that the kin in the West Indies comprise only a portion of the kin universes of participants, as do the kin in Los Angeles, the numbers are quite impressive.

Given the difficulties of sponsoring kinsmen for immigration, other than those in the categories of spouse, children, siblings, and parents, it is

not peculiar that so many kin have remained in the
homeland.   Neither is it peculiar to find such a
wide range of kin left behind.   There is depth of
kin networks ranging in kind from one to three
generations, and breadth ranging from uncles,
aunts, and cousins to second cousins.

INTERACTIONAL CONTENT OF TRANSNATIONAL KIN NETWORKS

Analysis of patterns of reciprocity and the
content of reciprocity of kin-based networks that
transcend national boundaries among Afro-
Trinidadians show clearly that interaction with
one's intimates does not cease with the crossing of
national boundaries.   Naturally, social interaction
will less often be of a face-to-face nature and
will most likely be less frequent, but it is not
necessarily of less emotional intensity.   Table 10
shows the content of interaction between sample
members in Los Angeles and kin in the West Indies,
including only the intimate zone.

Whereas 63 percent of the participants refused
to write letters to kin in North American cities,
80 percent (24) of them write to kin in the West
Indies.   However, five of them write as seldom as
once a year, and six of them write only once every
six months, while as many as eight write once a
month, but only a handful write every two weeks.

Even more surprising, 93 percent (28) of the
sample make international telephone calls to their
kin in Trinidad despite the exorbitant rates
charged.   Fifty percent of the sample call overseas
as often as once a month.   Thirty percent call
approximately twice a year, and 13 percent call
once a year, usually at Christmas.   Ian Nelson is
one of the frequent overseas callers.   Many sample
members corroborated his description of his long
distance and international telephone habits:

I mostly keep in touch with my brother in Miami
and my two younger brothers in Trinidad. ......
I talk to my brother in Miami almost every day,
and I telephone my younger brothers in Trinidad
quite often.   I just spoke to them the other
day.   I talk to my sister in Venezuela a couple
of times a year.   I keep in touch by phone.   I
don't write.   I hate writing.

Although remittances are clearly a much less
popular type of exchange, as many as 40 percent of
the participants are engaged in this form of
reciprocity; in nine of the twelve cases, such
reciprocity takes the form of sending money every
three or four months to the participant's mother or
mother-figure in Trinidad or other territories in
the West Indies.   As other scholars have noted,
remittances are usually used by recipients to
purchase either daily necessities, such as food, or
luxury items, such as expensive furniture, and not
for investment in savings or other productive
enterprises (Rubenstein 1983).   Two of the
participants involved in remittance exchange were
recipients rather than senders, and one of the
cases involved both receiving and sending, less
common situations than sending remittances which is
a centuries-old tradition among migrants across the
globe.
    Patsy Archer has been both a recipient and a
sender of remittances.   Prior to migration, Patsy
received remittances from Neville, her lover who
had migrated to Los Angeles 4 years earlier.   She
had remained behind with their four children.   They
were not married at the time of his departure.
Actually, Patsy was supposed to receive the
remittances on a regular basis from Neville's older
brother, who had been delegated responsibility for
Patsy and the children.   Neville's older brother
did not live up to his responsibilities.   Patsy
received some, but by no means all, of the
remittances.   When Patsy and Neville were re-united
and married in Los Angeles 4 years after Neville

left, he had to show her the money order receipts to prove to her he had sent them.

When Patsy migrated, she became a sender of remittances because she had left all four children, ranging in age from 4 to 11 years, to be looked after by her aunt, her mother's sister. The circumstances of her migration were such that she could not bring the children with her at the time, so she worked and sent money to her aunt for the children's care. Her aunt kept the four children for 3 years until Patsy got her "green card" and Patsy was able to send for the children. Patsy is still very close to her aunt because both of Patsy's parents, as well as her siblings, died when she was a young girl, and she was looked after by her aunt during her childhood. Patsy expresses her gratitude to her aunt by writing regularly, even though she hates letter writing, and keeping in touch by phone, as well as inviting her aunt to come to Los Angeles on vacation and to stay as a houseguest for as long as she wishes.

In some cases, but by no means all of them, there appears to be an association between the sending of remittances and the receipt of child care services in exchange. The case of Patsy Archer, just described, is one such instance. Another case discussed earlier in this chapter, that of Neil and Heather Johnson, her two sons, and her mother, deserves mention again because they enlisted the help of Neil's mother and grandmother in the U.S. Virgin Islands to look after their daughter, Tamara. Shortly after Tamara was born, Heather decided it was time to finish her secondary education, which was incomplete when she left Trinidad and Tobago, and to acquire a skill that paid well. Heather needed someone to look after infant Tamara while she was at school. Neil was unavailable, as he was working full time, and her two older sons were too young to take care of an infant, so Heather sent Tamara off to the U.S. Virgin Islands to spend the first year of her life there with her grandmother and great grandmother. Tamara came back to Los Angeles after a year, but

Heather and Neil keep in close touch by phone with his mother and grandmother and send regular remittances.   There is also visiting back and forth: Neil spent a month there in 1981, then his grandmother came to Los Angeles for Christmas in 1983 and spent 3 months as a house guest.

The case of Linda Arundell also illustrates the kinds of ties that continue to bind Afro-Trinidadians to their homeland.   Linda left Trinidad and Tobago 12 years ago, leaving her young son, Winfield, who was five years old at the time, in the care of her mother and sisters.   In New York, she met Courtney with whom she fell in love, and they moved in together and had two sons.   They decided to get married when the second boy was two years old and a few years later decided to move to Los Angeles.   For the past 12 years, her oldest son, Winfield, has been looked after by his grand-mother in Trinidad and Tobago.   After Linda and Courtney and their sons settled in Los Angeles, she sent for Winfield to come and live with them.   By then, Winfield was about 17 years old.   He spent one summer with his mother, stepfather, and half-siblings and decided he hated it and went back to Trinidad to live with his grandmother and aunts. Linda used to visit Trinidad at least once a year while living in New York but has not continued this pattern since moving to Los Angeles because it is more expensive.   But, in spite of the expense, Linda will continue to have persisting obligations that link her to her kin in Trinidad.

The last three cases described are really examples, of "child-fostering", a tradition with a long history in the Caribbean.   "Child-fostering" may be defined as the informal and temporary transfer of parental rights and duties to kin other than biological parents or to trusted friends who assume responsibility for the care of the child/children.   It differs from the North American custom by the same name in that it does not involve intervention by State or other bureau-cracies, or placement in the home of a stranger.   West Indian children are usually "fostered" by those already

well-known to the child and of whom the child is
very fond. Nor does it involve the legal "red
tape" or permanence of North American adoption.
"Child-fostering" among Afro-Trinidadians in Los
Angeles is similar to the Caribbean custom except
that it has been made international in scope by
international migration. It is therefore a form of
international reciprocity that cements, par
excellence, the ties that continue to bind
Trinidadian migrants to their homeland, as
evidenced by the fact that one-third of the sample
are currently or were in the past involved in such
arrangements.

A different type of bond linking seven sample
members to kin in Trinidad and Tobago is owning
property in common with them in Trinidad and
Tobago. Except in the case of Ralph Gonzalez,
whose property consists of land, as well as two
houses, one in the capitol city and one at the
beach, most of the other property owned by
participants is in the form of land only. Owning
land in contemporary Trinidad and Tobago is nothing
to ridicule. In a brief analysis of current
economic developments in Trinidad and Tobago,
Braveboy-Wagner (1983) observed that Trinidad and
Tobago had been declared a "modern" society by the
Overseas Development Council, a private "think
tank" in Washington, D.C., because the oil crisis
and the "petrodollars" that flowed into Trinidad
and Tobago had conferred upon the country a per
capita GNP of over $3,500 and a Physical Quality of
Life Index score of more than 90. One of the
manifestations of this "modernity," among others,
was a scarcity of real estate and housing.

As one of the participants, Ian Nelson, put it:
"Land is skyrocketing down in Trinidad, you know."
Ian owns land in a rural district of Trinidad, not
in the capital city. Colin Dexter bought some land
in 1977 for $12,000 (TT) and sold it in 1980 for
$141,000 (TT).

Besides land, Ralph Gonzalez owns a house in
the capital city of Port of Spain and a beach house
in Northeastern Trinidad. He pays one of his

cousins to manage his property in his absence. He did not volunteer the value of his property, so I did not ask him for fear of offending him. Other participants volunteered all of the information about property values. It does not require much imagination, however, to guess at the worth of his properties. If real estate values seem high, the cost of housing is astronomical. In the capital city, I am told, houses in modern, middle-class neighborhoods cannot be had for less than $1/2million TT. In wealthier districts, they cost several $million TT. Ralph keeps in close touch with his uncles, aunts, and cousins and is their houseguest when he visits. He visited in 1973, 1974, 1979, 1981, 1982, and 1983.

TRANSCONTINENTAL AND INTERNATIONAL TRAVEL

Scholars of intra-national, rural-urban migration have observed that links between city and countryside persist, sustained by patterns of regular visiting by migrants to their home villages (Caldwell 1969). This is also true on an international level. Transcontinental and international visiting are two ways in which Afro-Trinidadians continue to be linked with social intimates in other cities of the host country, as well as with those in their countries of origin. Social interdependence between countries of origin and host countries, binding them into a common social field, is reinforced by other patterns of reciprocity delineated above. For example, letters, telephone conversations, remittances, child fostering and ownership of property in the homeland. But patterns of visiting are of a different order. For one thing, visiting involves face-to-face interaction, unlike the others mentioned. Afro-Trinidadians who are visiting their homeland not only meet with their intimates in person, but have a chance to observe the state of their country of origin, perhaps with return migration in mind.

Visiting kin in other cities in North America is practiced by all of the Afro-Trinidadian participants who have kin in these places as shown in Table 11. Only one visits as often as once a month, and another, twice a year. One-third of the sample visits once a year, 17 percent only every 2 years, and 23 percent only once every 3 or 4 years.

Apart from visits on a regular basis, usually for a vacation lasting anywhere from a few weeks to a month, there are also unplanned visits to attend life crisis events, such as funerals. Only one participant, Felix Coleman, has been back to New York since moving to Los Angeles, to attend his mother's funeral.

On these visits, Afro-Trinidadians are usually houseguests of the kin they visit. In fact, all of the twenty-four participants with kin are their kin's houseguests. Heather Johnson, for example, visits New York every year to see her mother, her brothers, and her best friend who lives there. She is always a houseguest of her mother. Heather, therefore, has to host relatives from New York when they come to visit her in Los Angeles. For instance, her mother comes to Los Angeles every year, as well as her brothers, two aunts and a cousin. However, although visiting is usually a reciprocal matter, not all relatives in other places come to Los Angeles to visit; therefore, participants are more often guests than hosts.

In spite of the high cost of round-trip airfare from Los Angeles to Trinidad and Tobago, 100 percent of the Afro-Trinidadian sample periodically visit their homeland on vacation. However, only one participant visits twice a year. Twenty percent visit as often as once a year, while 24 percent go only once every two years. The majority, (50 percent), only visit once every 3 to 7 yeaers, and one participant goes as infrequently as once every 10 years. Many secondary migrants from New York stated that when they lived in New York they used

to visit Trinidad and Tobago every year. Now they
cannot afford to go as often.

Gift-giving and visiting go hand in hand.
Visiting kin and close friends in Trinidad and
Tobago without gifts would be unforgivable. And
nowadays, kin in Trinidad are more demanding in
what they want for gifts with their newly-found
petrodollar affluence. They do not want trinkets.
What relatives demand as gifts is the latest in
electronic equipment, stereo components, color
televisions, videocassette recorders, microwave
ovens, refrigerators, and the like. The reason
these items are in such demand as gifts is that
their prices in Trinidad and Tobago, after import
tax and merchant mark-up have been added, are often
triple or quadruple the cost of the same items in
the U.S. Hence, those in the West Indies implore
their visiting relatives to bring such things
because even after 100 percent customs duties have
been charged, paying customs duties is still
cheaper than buying the item locally.

Of the annual visits, many choose to make them
either at Christmas or at Carnival time (2 days
before Lent). Christmas and Carnival are the two
most momentous events of the social calendar in
Trinidad and Tobago, and Carnival is the more
spectacular of the two. Only four, (13 percent),
of the participants choose to go home for
Christmas. One visits both at Christmas and at
Carnival. Whereas only a few visit Trinidad and
Tobago for Christmas, more than half the sample,
(53 percent) go home for Carnival and five of them
do so every year.

Carnival in Trinidad and Tobago is today the
paramount national festival. It is a spectacle so
colossal, it is only to be rivaled by Carnival in
Brazil. Although the latter is more famous world-
wide, Trinidadians of all races are obsessed with
Carnival in their homeland. Those living in
Trinidad and Tobago spend the entire year
organizing and preparing for the next one, in eager
anticipation. When Carnival finally arrives, the
two days before Lent are spent in non-stop,

marathon dancing to the music of steelbands, in
masquerade, in the streets for 48 hours. For weeks
beforehand, there is partying and dancing every
weekend, and many weekdays, to warm up for the big
event itself. Few can resist the temptation to be
home during this period of frenzied revelry. Colin
Dexter puts it this way:

> I go home every Carnival. How you mean? I
> can't miss dat! You know any medicine de
> doctor could give me to make me happy besides
> dat? Dat's the greatest ting in the world,
> man! You making joke or what? Talking about
> Carnival in Trinidad, boy? Sweet too bad! Rum
> drinking and ting!

Colin told me the reason he went into the real
estate business in the first place was because he
saw that it was a way to make a lot of money
quickly, in order that he could become independent.
It was not the money so much that he was after, as
the independence. Being Trinidadian, independence
for Colin meant having the freedom to go home for
Christmas and Carnival and to enjoy himself in ways
not possible in the U.S. He observed that in
Trinidad there are certain freedoms not available
in the United States, especially for a black man.
For instance, Colin mentioned freedoms such as
joking with the police and teasing them. Double
parking. Drinking in the the streets to the point
of "rolling in de canal" [passing out in the
gutter]. He loved it because when he did these
things in Trinidad, "nobody can't do you nutt'n."
In Trinidad, one is only arrested for serious
crimes, not hassled for petty offenses like
drinking in the streets or other minor infractions.
In Trinidad, one can pretty much do as one pleases
without being held accountable, particularly at
Carnival time. Other participants, mainly male,
had similar complaints when asked what they did not
like about life in the U.S.
   Ian Nelson and his black American wife go to
Trinidad and Tobago for Carnival every year also.

He described his wife as a "Trinidad fan". Since they have been together, they have never missed a Carnival. He told me excitedly about their plan to spend 3 weeks there partying by night and going to the beach by day, without interruption. He said he had spoken to his brothers on international telephone, and they had arranged it so that everyone could go directly to a party as soon as they cleared customs in Trinidad. Not just Ian and his wife and his brothers and their wives, but also Ian's best friend in Los Angeles, also a Trinidadian, his best friend's girlfriend and his best friend's brothers and their wives, en masse. While in Trinidad, Ian and his wife are usually houseguests of his mother, although sometimes they stay at one of his brothers. He delights in the company of his family for this brief period. During his visit, he also drops by and "limes" with some of his old friends from school days, who have moved back to Trinidad, and they spend time leisurely "ole-talking" and catching up with what has happened in each other's lives during the year since they last saw one another.

Rupert Sinclair also catches the fever at Carnival time, as he related to me:

I was in Trinidad recently for Carnival. I love to go for Carnival. I have a lot of fun. Maureen (his wife) doesn't get too much of a kick out of it, but I love to go and "hang out" with my friends. Whatever part of the globe I'm in, I like to be in Trinidad at Carnival time.

Apart from Carnival visits, there are other festive reasons for going home, such as the wedding of a relative. Only two participants have done this during the period of my research as shown in Table 11. There are also more somber reasons for returning, such as serious illness or perhaps even a funeral. Only four participants did this in the course of my research (see Table 11). As in the case of transcontinental visiting, returning home, for all of the sample members, automatically implies being a houseguest of kin who have remained in Trinidad (see Table 11). In turn, being a houseguest implies hosting these same relatives when they become the travellers and visit the U.S. However, not all who visit also host in return, as some relatives in Trinidad are reluctant to leave home and travel, as shown in Table 11. With all this traveling back and forth, it might be said that Afro-Trinidadians practice "international shuttling."

In this long discussion of kin-based networks of the Afro-Trinidadian sample, I have tried to stress that kinship, of all the primary relationships possible, seems to be the most enduring and reliable, although not in every case. But more importantly, I wish to make the point that the maintenance of these kin-based ties by the participants involves an element of choice. That is to say, kin obligations for Afro-Trinidadians are not of the ascribed, fixed variety associated with membership in a corporate descent group.

Personal acts of choice are implied in maintaining access to bilateral kin, particularly when kinsmen move from the intimate to the effective zone and vice versa. However much kinship relations may naturally wax and wane over time, it requires concerted effort to sustain these links. Their very existence implies bonds of an achieved nature that have taken on a voluntary character, not unlike that of friendship. It is to friendship and other types of associations that I shall turn in the next chapter.

CHAPTER VII

TRANSNATIONAL AND TRANSCONTINENTAL FRIENDSHIP NETWORKS

In an earlier chapter, I suggested that kin-based relations have by nature an obligatory quality, being the product of institutional pressures toward permanence which are exerted on members of ascribed kin groups. In contexts of bilateral kinship, as is the case here, an element of choice exists to the extent that one may select those kin with whom one wishes to interact. Kinship is nevertheless an ascriptively-based social relationship. In contrast, friendship is entirely voluntary and thus is a relationship forged out of achievement (Litwak & Szelenyi 1969; Wolf 1966). Precisely because of its voluntary and emotional character, the strength of friendship ties is more ephemeral and susceptible to the dynamics of change. For example, a shift in residence and concomitant interruptions in face-to-face contact may result in the complete rupture of friendship ties, or the "out of sight, out of mind" phenomenon.

However, geographical mobility need not necessarily lead to the dissolution of friendship. As Jacobson (1971) argued compellingly, friendship is often based on expectations of continuity rather than on ongoing, frequent contact. Although only intermittently activated because of interruptions brought about by changes in location, friendships

127

of the geographically mobile persist and endure by
virtue of encapsulation in a system of expections
instead of interactions (Jacobson 1971). Indeed,
Jacobson (1971) demonstrated that highly mobile
individuals tend to form quick, intimate
relationships with friends of mutual friends to
whom they have been referred. These strong,
emotional friendships become latent and dormant
when people move, to be reactivated at some future
date when time and geography permit. More
commonly, then, changes in residence bring about
changes in network structure, such as fluctuations
in the size and density of friendship networks,
changes in density of network sectors, shifts of
friends from one zone of interaction to another
(e.g., intimate to effective), as well as
transformations in content.

FRIEND-BASED NETWORKS IN THE WEST INDIES

A shift in residence as drastic as moving
thousands of miles away from one's close associates
is bound to produce changes of various kinds in the
friendship patterns of the participants. Since
friendship is founded entirely on free choice, it
is up to each migrant to decide whether to maintain
or sever relations with those left behind. The
most extreme option would be the complete rupture
of ties, resulting in the total absence of
friendship links with the West Indies. Four
participants in the research sample have chosen
this extreme (See Table 12). One of them was Felix
Coleman, who justified his action in this way:

I don't keep in touch with anyone. I don't
correspond with anybody. A lot of the people I
went to school with, I don't know where they
are. Many went away. Some are in Canada,
England. Those who stayed have done exactly
what was expected of them: go to school, get a

G.C.E. pass,get a job.   They haven't done
anything else.   They go home after work and
party and drink and womanize and stay at that
pace.   It may sound like boasting, but I have
nothing to say to the people I knew in
Trinidad.

A less drastic consequence of emigration is a
contraction in the size of friendship networks. As
Table 12 shows, almost half of the sample, 14
participants, have only a small number of intimate
friends, between one and four individuals,
remaining in the West Indies.   Another twelve
participants have a greater number of intimate
friends in the West Indies, ranging in number from
five to ten.   The preservation of intimate ties
with friends in the West Indies by the majority of
participants does not appear to be related to the
factors of age, gender, socio-economic status or
length of residence abroad.   Rather, it appears to
be partly a function of a strong sense of
commitment to a special sort of bond between
individuals, involving mutual obligations, and not
simply sociability, which demands only superficial
acquaintance.   I believe it is this sense of
commitment which Jacobson (1971) was referring to
when he suggested that friendship links can be
based on expectations of continuity rather than
frequent interaction.

Patrick Inniss, one of the research
participants, defined a friend, as distinct from an
acquaintance, as "someone in whom I can trust with
a certain amount of confidence and can depend on in
case of emergency.   And it should be a reciprocal
thing."   Mutual aid and the exchange of goods and
services, then, are also implied in friendship.
One participant lent $1000 (U.S.) to a friend in
Trinidad and Tobago over a year ago. This loan has
not been repaid, much to the anger of the
participant, attesting to the fact that mutuality,
although ideal, is not always real.

Enduring friendship ties, however, must be
renewed by occasional contact, however sporadic and

in whatever form. Those participants with close
friends remaining in the West Indies visit them
from time to time. Frequency of visiting ranges
from twice a year to once every three years, the
majority averaging visits once a year. In short,
friendships need to be re-activated from time to
time. The natural course of friendship is
characterized by fluctuation in the intensity of
relations over time. When a move over vast
distances and national boundaries is introduced
into the situation, questions of latency emerge.

For example, how long can friendship ties lie
dormant and still be easily re-activated? Direct
contact between participants and their close
friends in the West Indies occur on an average of
once a year. This seems to be sufficient to
maintain intimacy and trust among the sample
members. In addition, close friendships may
persist and endure through time despite infrequent
interaction. The relationships of the participants
with their friends in the West Indies ranged in
duration from 7 to 52 years.

With each move of the Afro-Trinidadian sample,
the size of friendship networks has diminished and
there has also been a reduction in the density of
those networks. Density is calculated as the ratio
of total possible links to the total actual links
in any personal network (Boissevain 1974:39).
Density is a measure of the extent to which links
which could exist among persons do in fact exist
(Mitchell 1969:18), and it indicates what
proportion of those who know ego also know one
another and are in touch with each other
independent of ego. Density is, thus, an
expression of potential communication between
members of a network and therefore of the quantity
and quality of information exchanged. But, as
Boissevain (1974) is quick to point out, it does
not necessarily follow that "where contact, there
communication." A more accurate corollary would be
"where contact, there possible communication." As
Table 13 shows, the density of friendship networks
in the West Indies, which was 82.6 percent, dropped

to 73.5 percent in other cities of North America
and is only 64.5 percent in Los Angeles. This is
partly due to the migration of participants and
partly to the migration of other members of their
networks.

Another change that has taken place in the
friendship networks of the research participants is
the movement of friends from one zone of
interaction to another. As mentioned earlier, four
participants no longer have any close friends in
the West Indies. Prior to their migration, these
individuals most certainly had friends in the
intimate zone. Since the move, these once close
friends have moved from the intimate to either the
effective or extended zones. Those friends who
were once bound to these four participants by
strong emotions still have warm relations with them
but are bound less by emotion than by instrumental
concerns, which Boissevain (1974) defines as the
effective zone. Those friends who occupy the
extended zone are ones with whom the participants
have only superficial contact. Many are simply
acquaintances or friends of friends (Boissevain
1974).

With respect to friends in the West Indies,
much of the zone movement is from the intimate to
the effective zone, but not vice versa. A few also
move from the effective to the extended zone, but
most contacts in the extended zone were already
there to begin with. Zone movement in the opposite
direction seldom occurs, if ever.

Bert Diamond's account of how he spent his time
on a recent trip to Trinidad and Tobago for
Carnival illustrates the shift of friends from one
zone to another, as well as the casual nature of
the interaction that characterizes relationships in
the extended zone, which includes most friendship
links in the West Indies:

That's how I spend my Carnival. . . I sit there
and drink and talk with friends I haven't seen
for years. . . You see so many other people who
are visiting from being away like yourself. . .

You run into someone you haven't seen for 5
years, you start a conversation. . . all you're
trying to do is make up for those 5 years. As
soon as you walk away, you run into somebody
else you haven't seen for so long. And so it
keeps going in a circle. You keep running into
people and talking.

It is not that one does not drink and talk with
close friends.   Clearly that is not the case.
Rather, the major difference between intimate
relations and those in the extended zone is that,
in the latter, interaction is based on chance
encounters and fleeting contact, with no future
commitment in mind.   On the other hand, intimate
relations involve future expectations and mutual
obligations. For instance, Bert stated that he was
expecting some very good friends from Trinidad and
Tobago, with whom he keeps in sporadic contact, to
visit as his house guests in Los Angeles during the
1984 Olympic Games.   He felt obliged to show them
around Los Angeles to reciprocate for courtesies
extended to him during his visits back home.
The most dramatic transformations in the West
Indian friendship networks, as a result of the
participants' emigration, has been the changes in
interactional content. When sample members lived
in Trinidad and Tobago, interaction with their
close friends included a wide variety of
recreational pursuits, as well as mutual aid and
services.   Migration has reduced interaction to a
narrow repertoire which includes the occasional
exchange of letters, rare telephone conversations,
and visits ranging in frequency from twice a year
to once every 3 years.
It is during these periodic visits that the
previous quality of interaction is most closely
approximated.   However, because it happens
infrequently, there is pressure to condense as much
as possible into a short period of time.
Participants are seldom houseguests of their
friends (only two cases) as they usually stay with
their relatives.   Therefore, they commonly go and

"look for" (look up) their friends, dropping by and "liming." They sit around and drink and "ole talk," catching up with news of each other, as well as with gossip about others in their networks, since the last contact. Roderick Philips described his social interaction with some close friends on a recent visit and the changes he observed in them, which he attributed to their newly-found affluence as a result of the influx of "petrodollars" in the Trinidad economy:

> I found some friends were drinking too much. There is an affluence. I would have had much more money if I had remained in Trinidad, but I would be drinking more. When I went home, they want to kill me with alcohol. Just a little "lime" and they want to buy whisky. They have the money, like they don't know what to do with it. I don't want to get hooked into a circle of friends who all they know how to do is to drink and party. I like to party and I like to drink, but not like I see them doing, every day of the week. Things have not remained stagnant as when we left them. The Trinidad that we knew is completely different now. Young people like myself are talking about loans of $400,000 and $500,000 to build a house. I met my contemporaries talking some dollars that would blow your mind. Getting into debt, it ent [aint] no big thing. Husband and wife each have a car, kids have bicycles and you wondering where they get all this money from.

In summary, only a few members of the Afro-Trinidadian sample have chosen to sever ties with close friends in the West Indies. The majority of the participants (87%) continue to keep up close friendships with a small to moderate number of friends left behind. Although there have been dramatic changes in the content of interaction, as well as the frequencies of interaction, it would appear that frequent contact is not a requirement of enduring friendship ties, as some scholars have suggested. Rather, what is required appears to be a strong sense of commitment to a bond based on expectations of continuity, however infrequently re-activated.

FRIEND-BASED NETWORKS IN NORTH AMERICA

With six exceptions, members of the Afro-Trinidadian sample maintain intimate friendship ties with persons living in New York, New Jersey, Washington D.C., Boston, Miami, Oakland, Montreal, Toronto, and Hartford, Connecticut. As one might expect, secondary migrants from other cities in North America would naturally have made friends in the various cities in which they previously resided, and it is not surprising that some of these relationships have been maintained following the move to Los Angeles. In addition, five individuals who have not lived elsewhere in North America, have friends in some of these cities, even though they themselves have never lived there. This is particularly true of New York, Toronto, Miami, and Washington, D.C.

There are several reasons for this seeming paradox. First, these friendships obviously began back in the homeland prior to migration and have persisted. Second, they are also relationships between parties both of whom have migrated from a single point of origin to different destinations. New York, Toronto, and Miami are very popular destinations for West Indians. West Indian emigration being the institution that it is, it is not at all uncommon to find that friends of an individual migrant have migrated as well, some to the same destination, others to different ones. The enduring friendships of the five participants derive from various sources. A few are fellow musicians and fellow sportsmen. Others are former co-workers. Most continuing relationships are drawn from the categories of former schoolmates and "family friends."

By "family friend," I mean "those persons who are friends with each other as a result of being members of kin groups that have known each other and been on friendly terms for two or more generations." To illustrate, Yvette Harris and Marilyn Price are "family friends." Yvette and Marilyn used to live in the same general area in Trinidad. They have known each other and have been friends since they were small children. Yvette and Marilyn went to the same primary school. Their parents have been friends as long as either of them can remember. The two families have been close for quite some time. Both families migrated to New York (although at different times) and remained friends in New York. Yvette and her husband decided to move to Los Angeles and encouraged Marilyn to do the same. Marilyn did so a year or two later and brought her mother and many siblings, as well as siblings' spouses and children, along with her. Yvette and Marilyn remain close friends today, although their friendship has had its ups and downs. There were periods when they did not get along, but they are now back on speaking terms.

Yvette Harris' best friend is Marilyn Price's first cousin, Jackie, who lives in Toronto. Apart from the two kin groups being acquainted with each other, Yvette and Jackie are best friends because they were classmates. They attended the same secondary school. Although Jackie moved to Toronto and Yvette to New York, and later to Los Angeles, they keep in touch by letter and occasional telephone calls. Before Yvette moved from New York to Los Angeles, she used to visit Jackie periodically in Toronto. Since Yvette's second move, they have only seen each other once, when Jackie visited Los Angeles and was Yvette's houseguest for a couple of weeks about 3 years ago. They are not in contact as frequently as they once were, but their feeling for each other remains strong even though they are separated by long distances.

Earlier it was indicated that six participants have no close friends in other cities of North America (see Table 12). This is only partly the outcome of ruptured friendship ties with fellow islanders who migrated to other destinations. It is also a function of the fact that these six primary migrants have not lived elsewhere in North America and thus have had no other contexts for making new acquaintances. This contrasts sharply with the twenty secondary migrants who have lived elsewhere, all of whom chose to pursue close friendships with persons who derive from their country of origin, and who, in turn, migrated to other destinations in North America. These intimate friends living elsewhere in North America derive mainly from the categories of former schoolmates, "family friends," and a few former co-workers. Thus, many old relationships persist.

Other intimate friends in cities of North America consist of newly acquired ones made in the course of residing in these other cities. With each step of migration, it is only natural for new friendships to be formed, recruited from new sources. One new source of friendship would be migrants from regions of the homeland different from one's own original locality, whose acquaintance one would make following migration to the same destination. Another new source of friendship would be migrants from other West Indian nations who shared the same destination. Prior to migration, sample members would seldom have known many other types of West Indians except for those intra-regional migrants to Trinidad from smaller Eastern Caribbean islands such as Barbados, Grenada, and St. Vincent.

Yet another source of new friendships would include Americans, natives of the country of destination, encountered on an equal basis for the first time after the arrival of participants to the new country. Back home, the only Americans they would have come in contact with would have been tourists with whom they most likely would not have interacted. New relationships may also be

recruited from new activity fields, such as fellow
workers, friends of old friends, fellow schoolmates
(for those who continued their education post-
migration), and U.S. Army "buddies" (for two
participants who joined the U.S. Army post-
migration). Thus, for the first time, sample
members who were primary migrants to other cities
in North America were introduced to people from a
variety of national origins and to new activity
fields peopled by individuals quite different from
their previous associates.

Secondary migration of participants from other
cities of North America to Los Angeles has brought
about changes in the structure of their friendship
networks in these cities of previous residence.
One such change is the shift of friends from one
zone of interaction to another, chiefly from the
intimate zone to the effective zone, and in a few
cases, to the extended zone. As before, movement
has tended to be unidirectional, for example, from
intimate to effective: reverse movement seldom
occurs, particularly following changes of residence
involving long distances. These shifts from the
intimate to the effective zone leave "vacancies,"
so to speak, in the intimate zone that may be
filled by new friends in the new place of
residence.

A contraction in the size of intimate
friendship networks to about two-thirds of their
former size has followed secondary migration of
participants to Los Angeles from other cities of
North America. As Table 12 shows, the number of
close friends which the Afro-Trinidadian sample
maintains in other cities of North America ranges
from one to fifteen. Although six have none at
all, three research participants still have between
one and four close friends in other North America
cities, while more than half the sample have
between five and ten such friends. Only a handful
have as many as eleven to fifteen close friends in
other parts of North America. This atrophy of the
intimate zone is primarily due to the shift of
friends from the intimate to the effective zone.

The density of intimate friendship networks with people in other cities of North America has been affected by the reduction in size and has atrophied as well (see Table 13). Whereas density of friendship networks in the West Indies was 82.6 percent, in North American cities other than Los Angeles, it is only 73.5 percent. This reduction in density is partly the result of friends being recruited from a greater variety of sources and the lack of multiplex relationships, with little overlap of activity fields.

As was the case for intimate friendship networks in the West Indies, changes in the interactional content of relations with friends elsewhere in North America following the participants move to Los Angeles have been most dramatic. Whereas sample members previously shared a gamut of pleasurable activities, as well as mutual aid with their friends when they lived in the same city, their relationships now consist mostly of an exchange of letters once every 2 to 3 months, telephone conversations every few months, and face-to-face visits ranging from once a year to once every 5 years. A few participants share job market information with one another. Some are houseguests when they visit these friends in other cities. In return, when these friends from out of town visit Los Angeles, the participants act as hosts and welcome these friends as guests in their homes. During these face-to-face visits (usually on vacation for one or two weeks), they spend their time "liming," "ole talking," drinking, and partying. They try to make up for the lapse in time since they were last face-to-face and catch up on each other's lives, enjoying each other's company.

While this is not true of all members of the sample, several participants have best friends who live far away in other cities. The case of Yvette Harris and her best friend in Toronto was described earlier. Janet Price is another example. She told me that what she missed most about the New York/New Jersey area were her friends. She has more close

friends back East than she does in Los Angeles, and
her two closest friends live in New Jersey. Except
for one friend whom she knew in Trinidad and
Tobago, she met the others, who are also
Trinidadian, in New Jersey after she migrated to
the eastern United States. Heather Johnson's best
friend also lives in New York and she laments the
distance that separates them:

> We don't talk (on the telephone) that often and
> we only see each other about once a year, but
> there is this closeness between us. I've known
> her for about 15 years. She lives in New York,
> and she's from Trinidad. I met her when I went
> to work for a bank in New York. I didn't know
> her back in Trinidad. . . . When it came time
> to say goodbye, we broke down in tears. It was
> very sad. She was the type of person I could
> talk to about everything. . . We talk to each
> other now and then on the phone. She was out
> here about a month ago. She comes out (to Los
> Angeles) about every other year. I go back to
> New York every year. So we see each other
> quite often.

To summarize, six sample members (20%) have no
close friends in other North American cities.
These are individuals who have never lived in any
other city in North America except Los Angeles, and
have not made the acquaintance of residents in
other cities. In contrast, the majority of the
sample (80%) maintain close relationships with
friends in other North American cities. A few of
these friends were known to the participants in the
homeland, and they derive from the domains of
"family friends," former schoolmates, and former
co-workers. Most, however, were newly recruited
following migration. The move to North America
broadened sample member's horizons by exposing them
to people from different regions of their homeland,
as well as to people from other nations in the West
Indies. It also placed them alongside natives of
the receiving country and made it necessary to

interact with them. Hence, for the first time,
participants in the research found themselves in a
multicultural setting of greater variety than they
had previously experienced.

FRIEND-BASED NETWORKS IN LOS ANGELES

The rewards of investigating the primary social
relationships of individuals are many, as
demonstrated by Keefe (1980) in her comparative
study of Mexican immigrants, native-born
Mexican-Americans, and Anglo-Americans in Southern
California. One virtue of such a research strategy
is that it makes possible a concept of "community"
that contrasts sharply with studies of "community"
premised on "place" phenomena. The superiority of
an approach conceived in interactional, rather than
spatial, terms is particularly striking in
metropolitan areas such as Southern California
where populations are spatially dispersed and where
there is often an absence of strong neighborhood
ties. Consequently, Keefe (1980) utilized the
concept of "personal community," defined as "the
total network of primary social relationships
maintained by an individual," to make sense of the
social life of her sample which appeared to be
organized according to principles of interaction
rather than space.

The results of this study have bearing on this
research with Afro-Trinidadian immigrants, as she
found significant differences between ethnic groups
and between Mexican immigrants and native-born
Mexican-Americans in the composition of their
"personal communities." For instance, she found
that the social networks of Mexican immigrants were
smallest in size and consisted almost entirely of
fellow immigrants, with equal numbers of kin and
friends (Keefe 1980:59-65).

In contrast, native-born Mexican-Americans had
the largest social networks, made up primarily of

kin.   Although their friends were predominantly
Mexican-Americans, their friendship networks were
more ethnically mixed than those of the immigrants
in that they included a few Anglo neighbors and
co-workers.   On the other hand, Anglo-American
sample members had relatively small social
networks, based almost exclusively on friendship
with fellow Anglo-Americans. For all three groups,
relationships with neighbors were relatively
unimportant (Keefe 1980:59-65).

These findings raise interesting questions
about the Afro-Trinidadian immigrant "community" in
Los Angeles and the composition of the "personal
communities" of sample members.   For example, are
their social networks in Los Angeles kin-based or
friend-based?   Are their friendship networks
ethnically mixed, or are they made up exclusively
of fellow Trinidadians?   Do they maintain close,
intimate ties with co-workers and neighbors?
Individuals within any personal network are usually
drawn from more than one activity field, for
example, the domains of kin, friends, co-workers,
and neighbors.   To what extent are these various
sectors kept separate? Or are they connected with
one another?   For example, are their social lives
compartmentalized or are they well-integrated?   Is
there overlapping of sectors (multiplexity)?   If
so, which sectors overlap most often?   What is the
average density within each sector?

The size of the friendship networks in Los
Angeles of the Afro-Trinidadian sample is shown in
Table 12. It should be recalled that these figures
include only the intimate zone. A comparison of
Table 12 with Table 8 is necessary in order to
determine whether the Los Angeles social networks
of the sample are kin-based or friend-based.   The
comparison of the two tables reveals a general
tendency toward equal numbers of kin and friends in
the Los Angeles context.   It should be stressed
that this equal distribution of kin and friends
seems to obtain only in the Los Angeles setting.

Comparing Table 8 with Table 12 shows that kin
outnumber friends in other cities of North America,

and the same is true of the intimate zone in the
West Indies.   Indeed, kin are about twice as
numerous in these other two contexts.   Thus, it
would appear that migration has reduced the
importance of kinship as a basis for intimate
relations in Los Angeles, relative to friendship.
At the same time, friendship is gaining in
significance in Los Angeles and has become of equal
importance to kinship.   This seems to conform with
the findings of Keefe (1980), as the immigrant
component of her sample had equal numbers of kin
and friends, but exclusively from their own ethnic
group.   This was in contrast to native-born
Mexican-Americans, whose social networks were more
ethnically mixed but consisted mainly of kin.
Anglo-Americans had social networks composed
exclusively of fellow Anglo-Americans and mainly of
friends, no kin.   Today, in terms of the relative
importance of kinship and friendship in the lives
of the Afro-Trinidadian sample members, each
appears to be equal.   Only time will tell if one
will gain priority over the other.

     In her insightful essay on network density,
Cubitt (1973) pointed out that it may be more
fruitful for network analysts to examine the
density of portions of networks that appear to
cluster, rather than to assess the overall density
of the total personal network.   In Cubitt's view,
properties of networks may not apply uniformly to
all segments of the network.   Therefore, measuring
the whole may actually distort the picture by
masking differences in its constituent parts
(Cubitt 1973:67).   She found in her research on 35
couples in Edinburgh, Scotland, that overall
network density was generally quite low, but there
were "sectors" of high density.   A "sector" is
defined as "a part of a network in which ego has an
analytically equivalent relationship with all
members of it" (Cubitt 1973:70).   Thus, density
most likely will be highest within sectors and
lowest for the entire network.   For instance,
kinship, by nature, is a sector of high density
(Cubitt 1973:70).

However, Cubitt (1973) cautioned that the concepts of social role and social field ought not to be confused when using a sector as a unit of analysis. For example, ego may have different relationships with different members of a social field, but the relationships of these members of one field with ego are analytically equivalent. Clusters within networks ought to be defined in terms of fields rather than roles. For example, a neighbor and an old school friend may each relate to ego in the role of confidante, but the sharing of this role does not enhance the probability that the neighbor and the old school friend will know one another. In contrast, two old school friends who share a field-type link are more likely to be acquainted. Thus, clusters based on the sharing of a field-type link will manifest greater density than portions of the network which only share similar roles (Cubitt 1973:69).

For all of the above reasons, I decided to classify the social networks of participants into the following four sectors: (1) kinship, (2) friendship, (3) work associates, and (4) neighbors, rather than assess the overall density of each network. Table 13 shows the average density of each of the above sectors, in three geographic locations. Density was calculated for each sector of each personal network, using the formula presented in Boissevain (1974:39). The mean density of each sector was then calculated for the whole sample. It can be seen that the kinship sector has the highest density, as one might expect. The kinship tie seems to produce an extremely high level of connectedness. That is to say, those who are in a relationship of kin to ego and who live in Los Angeles all (100 percent) know one another, while only 98.3 percent of those kin who live elsewhere in North America know each other, and only 94.9 percent of kin living in the West Indies are acquainted.

The reason that less than 100 percent of those who are kin to ego in the West Indies know each other is because they are affinal kin. That is to say, some of those who are related to ego only through marriage do not know each other. On the other hand, friendship is a sector that is less dense than that of kinship, and its density decreases as one moves from the West Indies to Los Angeles. In other words, 82.6 percent of ego's friends knew each other in the West Indies, but that is true of only 64.5 percent of ego's friends in Los Angeles. The density of friendship networks in other cities of North America seems to lie between these extremes. It would appear that density of friendship networks has declined with each successive move. This concurs with Cubitt's observation that density is inversely related to geographical mobility (1973:71).

The work associates sector has relatively high density in all three locations, ranging from 90.3 in the West Indies to 85.9 in other cities of North America, to 80.4 in Los Angeles. This is not surprising as one would expect most people who work together and thus spend a great deal of time together to know one another, at least in the work setting. However, this should not be taken as a clear-cut sign of intimate friendship. Whether they are friends with one another outside of the work context is an altogether different matter. This is because friends tend to be recruited from different activity fields and consequently may not know each other, whereas work associates are drawn from a single activity field.

The fourth sector, that of neighbors, shows the most dramatic fall in density between the West Indies and Los Angeles. Whereas the density of the neighbor sector in the West Indies was 88.7 percent, falling to 67.8 percent in other cities of North America, the density of that sector in Los Angeles was only 12.1 percent! Relations with neighbors in Los Angeles thus appear to be an insignificant part of the social networks of the Afro-Trinidadian sample. Only three of the participants in the research admitted to having relationships with neighbors that went beyond the most casual of greetings. While they are not on hostile terms with their neighbors, they most certainly are not on close terms with them.

Apart from size and density, range is also an important property of social networks, particularly where friendship is concerned, as it reveals the social heterogeneity of the individuals making up the friendship networks. Range can also disclose the variety of activity fields from which friends are drawn, as well as the ethnic and racial composition of the Los Angeles friendship networks of the Afro-Trinidadian sample.

Of the activity fields from which intimate friends of the Afro-Trinidadian sample are drawn, neighbors comprise the least important source of recruitment of close friends (only 1 percent). As indicated earlier, sample members are not on intimate terms with their neighbors. Since most sample members who have lived in other cities of North America report having been on closer terms with their neighbors in these other cities, this behavior pattern may be unique to Southern California. Indeed, Keefe (1980) found a similar lack of intimacy between neighbors in her study of Mexicans and Anglos in Southern California. Such findings lead one to the conclusion that in Southern California, spatial ties of neighborhood are insignificant in the structure of personal networks.

Former schoolmates are another source from which friends of sample members derive, although they comprise only a small proportion (3 percent) of friends. However, it is worth observing that ties with old school friends have not been so much maintained as re-activated in the way described by Jacobson (1971) mentioned earlier in this chapter. Those participants who are friends in Los Angeles with former schoolmates have more or less run into them again by accident after having lost track of each other for many years. They have renewed their friendship because fate has thrown them together again. Former schoolmates by nature tend to be fellow Trinidadians because they went to school together there.

Family friends I defined earlier as "those persons who are friends with each other as a result of being members of kin groups that have known each other and been on friendly terms for two or more generations." Only 3 percent of the friends in Los Angeles of the Afro-Trinidadian sample fall into this category. The participants in the research admitted that they became acquainted with most of their friends in Los Angeles after moving here and knew very few of them either in another North American city or back in Trinidad and Tobago. Like former schoolmates, family friends, by definition, are also fellow Trinidadians and are persons known in the homeland.

Sports is an activity field from which a larger proportion of close friends (4 percent) are recruited than from those previously discussed, although most sample members do not actively participate in sporting activities. Most are only involved as spectators at team sports such as cricket, soccer and sometimes basketball. Cricket, in particular, is a sport that engages the enthusiasm of most English-speaking West Indian males, if only as spectators. It provides an arena for socializing regularly in a spirit of comraderie and fosters a sense of "community". I was told by Bert Diamond that in the early sixties, cricket as a leisure-time activity, was a great unifying force for the West Indians of several English-speaking nationalities who lived in Los Angeles. In those days, there were very few West Indians in Los Angeles, and they all knew one another and were close friends. There is not the same sense of "community" today as the population size has increased dramatically, and less people are known to each other.

In the 1960's, English-speaking West Indians played cricket with each other and with a handful of Englishmen in Griffith Park every Sunday. Although it is still played every Sunday, at a different park, cricket has become more international in outlook and embraces players from various countries. No longer are the players

predominantly Anglophone West Indian. For
instance, the players include East Indians,
Pakistanis, Sri Lankans, Australians, New
Zealanders, and Englishmen, in addition to West
Indians. This more cosmopolitan game has
introduced West Indians to cricketers of other
nationalities whom they might otherwise never have
met or befriended. Furthermore, these players
come from all walks of life. For example, there
are doctors as well as welders.

Soccer is another team sport of which West
Indians are fond. There is a local team in Los
Angeles made up exclusively of West Indians who
play with each other regularly. In addition, there
is another soccer team in the San Jose area also
made up exclusively of West Indians. These two
teams play matches against each other twice a year
in Los Angeles and twice a year in San Jose,
usually during major holidays such as Memorial Day
or July Fourth. These matches are considered
important events in the yearly calendar of West
Indians in both locations and are well attended by
large numbers of spectators from the West Indian
"community", which has an abiding passion for the
sport.

Not many of the close friends of the
Afro-Trinidadian sample are recruited from the
domain of work. Co-workers constitute only 10
percent of the friends of the Afro-Trinidadian
sample. This pattern contrasts with that found for
Anglo-Americans: work associates apparently
comprise a large proportion of their friendship
networks. For example, Keefe (1980) found in her
comparative study of Anglos and Mexicans that the
Anglo component of her sample had twice as many
friends who were also co-workers as the Mexican
component.

One participant, Ian Nelson, described his work
relationships in this way: "I don't have any close
friends at work. Now and then I may get together
with someone from work to play some sports, but not
a close friendship. I learned from previous
experiences." The sentiments of Ian Nelson can be

generalized to most of the other members of the sample. Only three participants reported close friendships with work associates that go beyond superficial friendliness in the workplace and extend into social interaction outside the work setting and into one another's homes. Thus, only a small part of the friendship networks of the Afro-Trinidadian sample is made up of work associates.

The greatest proportion of friends made in Los Angeles by the Afro-Trinidadian sample is recruited from the domain of friends of friends. In other words, sample members became acquainted with the majority of their friends (77 percent) through introduction by their own friends. Usually this takes place in a context of sociability and recreation. One's friends introduce one to others in settings such as parties, picnics, sporting events, card games, night clubs, public dances, and ethnic festivals. Since sample members attend these events regularly, it is possible for them to continually enlarge their friendship networks. The natural course of friendship, in any case, is for some friendships to remain the same while some new ones are made and others are allowed to decline. As sample members meet new people, new acquaintances are being added to the intimate, effective and extended zones, while old friends move from one zone to another.

ETHNIC AND RACIAL COMPOSITION OF FRIENDSHIP NETWORKS IN LOS ANGELES

As the most eloquent spokesman for the assimilation paradigm, Milton Gordon (1964) contended that with the dwindling of regional and rural-urban differences, the two remaining bases for the formation of subsocieties and subcultures would be social class and ethnicity. Of these latter two bases, he felt that class differences outweighed ethnic differences in importance.

Furthermore, in discussing the interaction of class and ethnicity, he formulated the useful concept of "ethclass," the significance of which lies in the fact that primary relationships tend to be confined to the ethclass (Gordon 1964).

The friendship behavior of members of the Afro-Trinidadian sample at times appears to conform to the ethclass principle and at other times appears to defy it. The evidence is thus contradictory. By and large, ethclass is the basis of friendship formation in the intimate zone of personal networks. That is to say, the most intimate friends of the sample members appear to be persons of the same "ethclass."

However, it is by no means clear whether class loyalty supercedes ethnic allegiance in all social interaction. The tug of war between the opposing forces of ethnicity and social class is not always easily resolved. The effective and extended zones of friendship networks include individuals in a variety of social positions. Particularly with respect to relationships with fellow islanders, sample members appear to form friendships with fellow Trinidadians from a wide range of social statuses. I have personally observed doctors socializing with auto mechanics. In these settings what seemed to matter most was the fact that they were members of the same ethnic group. For example, a West Indian man whom I met at an ethnic festival told me that he preferred to "hang out with other West Indians" and also that "one thing about over here, you have to be friendly with people you wouldn't think to associate with at home. But that's the way it is here."

In other words, in the Los Angeles context, it seems to be quite acceptable for individuals to be friends with people to whom one might not even speak, in the homeland, because of differences in class status. At first glance, this sort of behavior might appear to be a paradox, since it is well known by Caribbean scholars that social class distinctions and upward mobility are of paramount importance to West Indians.

One possible explanation of why asymmetry in social status is accepted by fellow ethnics in friending behavior in Los Angeles is that geographical mobility itself has wiped clean the slates of their individual personal histories. They can, therefore, treat each other as equals by tacit agreement because their respective ascriptive burdens, such as family background, are not known to each other.   Ignorance of personal liabilities enables them to assume similarity of status based on similarity of ethnicity and culture and to overlook possible differences in social status.   In other words, the color-class hierarchy of the West Indies has not been transplanted intact to America. In my opinion, the absence of the color-class hierarchy is due partly to the tabula rasa phenomenon and partly to the operation of American racism.   That is to say, under conditions of racism, it becomes more important to cultivate solidarity founded on racial likeness than to continue to observe distinctions in skin color which have no meaning to the practitioners of American racism.

In addition, what may also be happening is that conceptions of social class differences have altered with the migration.   In contrast to their homelands, where social position and status differentiation are clearcut and unambiguous, America is a land with vague and fluid social class boundaries.   Being transplanted to this context has affected the friending behavior of Afro-Trinidadians.   In a calypso song entitled Mas' in Brooklyn, the Mighty Sparrow eloquently described this phenomenon:

> You could be from St. Clair[3] or John-John[4]
> In New York all dat done.
> It ent have no "who is who,"
> New York[5] equalize you.

> The Mighty Sparrow (1968)

The critical point being made by the Mighty
Sparrow, however, is that America has equalized
West Indians.   In other words, whether one comes
from the West Indian upper class or the West Indian
lower class, once in America, previous status
differences recede into the distance, rendering
persons equal.   This equalizing influence can be
detected in the friendship patterns of the
Afro-Trinidadian sample.   In choosing friends to be
included in their personal networks in Los Angeles,
participants seem to use different criteria of
selection than they did before migrating.   For one
thing, being a fellow islander in the country of
origin was simply a given, whereas in the context
of the United States, ethnicity becomes a very
important consideration.   Table 14 shows the ethnic
membership of the close friends of the participants
in the research.   It can be seen that close to half
of the friends of the sample (46 percent) are
fellow Trinidadians.   Thus, fellow islanders rank
high as first preference for friends.   Second in
preference are fellow West Indians (29 percent),
mostly those from English- speaking regions of the
Caribbean, such as Jamaicans, Guyanese, Grenadians,
Barbadians, Virgin Islanders, and Belizeans and
Panamanians, the latter two being also
Spanish-speaking.

Race is another factor that has gained
prominence in the lives of West Indian immigrants.
The experience of migrating to the United States
has generated in West Indians generally, and
Afro-Trinidadians in particular, a heightened sense
of racial consciousness.   Coming from societies
with a three-tiered, color-class hierarchy in which
social class distinctions often dwarfed racial
considerations, they have entered a two-tiered
system of racial opposition that pits blacks
against whites.   Most of the participants in the
research admitted that until they came to the
United States, they had never before been exposed
to institutionalized racism as virulent and intense
as they have experienced in their day-to-day lives
in a variety of contexts: the police, jobs,

housing and schools, to name only a few. Colin
Dexter expressed it this way:

> I was exposed for the first time to racial
> discrimination. I didn't know what the term
> meant before. . . America, to this day, is
> still a bigot country. I don't care who don't
> like it, America to me today is a bigot
> country. Racism is alive and well. . . But the
> racial thing I've gotten used to. It doesn't
> bother me anymore. It is a terrible thing.
> When I say it doesn't bother me anymore, I mean
> I don't have to take my energy and deal with it
> per se, because I recognize the fact that it
> will destroy you. You have to be very strong,
> you see, to understand and live with this
> thing, you know.

Courtney Arundell also described his personal
experience with racism directed at him by former
friends:

> I used to hang out with these white guys. But
> if you have a white friend and you go to his
> house all the time and he realize that his
> sister like you, he cut you loose, man.

Bert Diamond related his reactions to overtures
of friendship by a white boss:

> Most places I've worked, I ended up with white
> bosses who want me to come to their homes on
> the weekend. I had one boss who lived in
> Malibu Canyon and invited me to his house
> almost every other weekend. I told him, you
> might be O.K., but you have neighbors around
> who may not like me. I might be driving up
> there and one of your neighbors throw a big
> rock at me. I would be to blame, I put myself
> in that position. So let's don't cause any
> embarrassment to anybody. I just wouldn't
> visit you.

In spite of the pervasiveness of racism in
America and its deleterious effects on the lives of
black immigrants, Afro-Trinidadians still find it
appealing to emigrate to the United States for both
instrumental and expressive reasons. From a
material perspective, the standard of living that
many have achieved in America would be unattainable
in the homeland were they to return at this time.
This is because there are no economic niches there
for them: they would not be able to find
comparable work, comparable pay or housing and
other amenities comparable to those they currently
possess in the U.S.

One of the participants in the research, Bert
Diamond, returned to Trinidad and lived there for 4
years after living in the United States for 14
years. He re-migrated to Los Angeles after the 4
year period when he realized that he had made a
mistake and that return migration was a failure.
During his stay, he discovered that for him to
acquire material things comparable to those
acquired years ago by colleagues who have never
left Trinidad, would have cost him "a pound and a
crown," as he put it. From the perspective of
social life, he found that except for the love of
drinking, he had little in common with friends who
had never left Trinidad.   There was also very
little to do in the way of social activities. He
got very bored with the monotomy of things and with
the provinicialism of Trinidad. He decided to
return to a more cosmospolitan country where
everyone did not know everyone else's business.
Racism, then, becomes the price one has to pay for
other things in life one considers more important.

Interestingly, racism directed against blacks
has not had identical effects on its victims in
different loci of practice. While institutional
racism exists both in the United States and in
Great Britain, scholars of the black immigrant
experience in Great Britain have noted that in that
context there has emerged a clearcut, unmistakable
cultural identity based on blackness (Midgett 1975;
Sutton & Makiesky 1975). The sequelae of migration

for West Indians in the United States have been quite different. Scholars of the Caribbean immigrant experience in the United States have observed a racial ambivalence (Coombs 1970; Foner 1978) and have attributed these different reactions to racism to the presence of a black American minority in the United States setting.

In particular, the presence of blacks in North America has provided a basis of comparison for observations about West Indians in North America and has prompted many of the latter to set themselves apart from the former and emphasize their "foreignness" (Foner 1978:229). On the one hand, black West Indians in the United States avoid a complete identification with blackness for fear of being stigmatized and thereby defeating their aspirations towards middle-class status. On the other hand, they feel tremendous sympathy and empathy with the plight of black Americans since they have personally been subjected to similar injustices. They therefore trend a tightrope between these two positions.

One of the participants in the research, Ralph Gonzalez, revealed this racial ambivalence in himself when he made contradictory statements in the same interview:

Black Americans have a funny way of thinking, so I don't usually hang with many of them, but I have a couple of them for friends. What I mean is they on this white man kick and the system. Like somebody owe them something. . .

Well, there's always a hassle with the system, with the white man. As a foreigner, you might get a slightly better break, but basically, once you're black, that's it. Housing, jobs, everything. . . A West Indian of Negro ancestry probably have a better chance than the average black American, but it's still a struggle. I was in the service and worked with them and saw them at their "best", like the rednecks. It was quite an experience in the Army. It

prepared me for this because it's the same
thing all over again, only no bums this time.
But I'm not discouraged. I can live with it.

Another participant, Kenneth Simpson, told me
of his college experiences, his initial encounters
with black Americans, and his later change in
attitude:

During my school days, it wasn't just schooling
I had to learn. It was learning to get along
with American blacks. It took me a long time
to understand why most American blacks walk
around with a chip on their shoulders and I
couldn't deal with it. . . Eventually, over the
years, I came to understand their chip on the
shoulder as I started to get the same chip.
For the first two or three years I was here, I
was more friendly with the white guys in
school. I went to their parties. By the third
year, I began drifting toward the black side.
I wasn't aware of it happening until one day I
thought, what happened to the guys I used to
hang out with?

Today, most of Kenneth Simpson's friends are
black, and many of them are American blacks. His
account, quoted above, illustrates changing
friendship patterns over time. More importantly,
it points to the evolution of a black
consciousness, shaped by American society, that
develops from an initial racial ambivalence into a
cultural identity in which race is a salient
feature. However, the racial ambivalence among
black West Indians is not a balanced one. The
scales are tipped toward consciousness of their
blackness. First, their frequent encounters with
racial discrimination do not permit them to lose
such consciousness. In response to a question
about what they disliked most in American life,
almost half of the sample volunteered accounts of
infuriating experiences with racist police

brutality and racist employment discrimination that threw them into a rage in the mere re-telling.

Second, many Afro-Trinidadians are meeting more and more black Americans, in the context of work, with whom they have much in common, and they are striking up friendships with these persons of similar status. In addition, Afro-Trinidadians are acquiring a taste for black American music. They have become very fond of disco, soul, and funk. These two sensibilities are merging. All of these conditions favor the growth of a group identity based on race.

Given these circumstances, it is not surprising that black Americans make up 21 percent of the friendship networks of the Afro-Trinidadian sample, while white Americans comprise only 2 percent. Many sample members, of both sexes, reported that they found most white Americans to be very unfriendly and cold. In short, they feel rejected by white America.

Latinos comprise an even smaller portion of the friendship networks of the Afro-Trinidadian sample (1 percent). I believe this situation is not so much a question of rejection, but one of language barriers. Language differences can be a major obstacle in social relations even when race is held constant. For instance, only one participant reported a casual acquaintance with someone Haitian. A few participants reported lukewarm relations with Latinos, mostly in the work context. Only one participant, who happens to be an ardent aficionado of salsa music, reported close relationships with Cubans and Puerto Ricans, but not with Mexicans. He stressed the Caribbean connection with Cubans and Puerto Ricans.

Asians seem to constitute an even tinier portion of the participants' friendship networks (0.5 percent). Five participants reported friendships with Filipinos whom they met at work. For the most part, these participants are nurses, as there is high Filipino representation in the nursing profession. Their reports of these friendships led me to believe that they were quite

friendly on the job but not very close outside of
work. Only one or two reported friendships with
Koreans and Hawaiians, and again, these
relationships tended to be confined to the work
context.

Only (0.5 percent) of the participants reported
friendships with South Asians, such as Indians,
Pakistanis, and Sri Lankans, made in the course of
playing cricket. Also made via the game of cricket
were friendships with Englishmen, Australians, and
New Zealanders. In sum, it can be seen from Table
14 that the friendship networks in Los Angeles of
the Afro-Trinidadian sample are ethnically mixed to
only a slight degree. The largest proportion of
friends consists of fellow islanders. Fellow West
Indians and black Americans also rank high in
preference. Members of other ethnic groups are
very insignificant.

THE CONTENT OF FRIENDSHIP NETWORKS IN LOS ANGELES

Recreation and sociability generally comprise a
far greater part of the basis of the friendship tie
than that of the kinship bond. Indeed, it is more
characteristic for friends to predominate over kin
in certain recreational pursuits, such as playing
music, playing sports, and playing a distinctively
Trinidadian card game called "All Fours." Also,
there are several types of entertainment that are
uniquely West Indian. For example, there are boat
rides, ethnic festivals, West Indian public dances
sponsored by voluntary organizations, and West
Indian nightclubs that cater exclusively to West
Indian tastes in music, dancing, food, drink, and
style of interaction. The latter consists of
drinking, "liming," and "ole-talking" with those
present, as well as dancing to "soca" and reggae
music furnished by D.J.s, or occasionally by live
bands. Soca is an upbeat version of calypso. Its
name derives from a fusion of "soul" and "calypso."

Rhythmically faster, it is more conducive to dancing. The agenda is similar on boat rides, the difference being that all of the above take place on board a steam ship that cruises Los Angeles Harbor for four to five hours during the course of an evening.

It might be argued, then, that the motives for participants in these latter pastimes can only be two-fold: to socialize with those already known, but more importantly, to make new acquaintances and enlarge one's extended and effective zones of friendship. Since the individuals present at these public events are drawn from all walks of life, it follows that acquaintances made in these contexts will also cover a wide range of socio-economic statuses. Again, what seems to matter in these settings is that others should share similar ethnic sensibilities. In particular, West Indian public dances and West Indian nightclubs are settings in which there is a certain warmth generated by the enjoyment of music and dancing, as well as shared styles of interaction, such as joking in a similar fashion. This sharing of styles of symbolic behavior creates bonds of West Indian-ness between those present and transcends status distinctions, at least during the course of the evening.

WEST INDIAN VOLUNTARY ASSOCIATIONS IN LOS ANGELES

Given the numbers of West Indians estimated to be living in the Los Angeles metropolitan area, it is somewhat surprising to find so few voluntary associations among them. McLaughlin (1981) found a similar scarcity in New York. I have been told that there is a Jamaican club and a Guyanese-American club, but none of the participants in the research belong to either of them and could not tell me much about either of them. I also know of a Belizean association and have met one of the officers of this organization. He told me it has a dual purpose: civic responsibilities, such as providing scholarships to needy students, and recreation in the form of dances and other social functions.

I have personal knowledge of only two organizations involving Trinidadians at the present time.   One is an association whose membership consists of a variety of West Indians, but primarily Jamaicans and Trinidadians, as well as black Americans.   The other organization is explicitly Trinidadian both in name and in spirit. It was founded in early 1982 but went dormant in late 1982 due to continuous friction among its members.

In the late spring of 1984, one of the officers of the second group resurrected the club under the original name, but without consulting any of the founding members, and recruited new members and officers to fill vacant slots.   Needless to say, this behavior offended the original officers and members, particularly since this individual, who took it upon herself to revive the group, had always been very autocratic and had been the source of much of the friction within the original group. The result was much ill feeling toward this person and cleavage between the original members and newly recruited ones.   It is also interesting that whereas the original members were mostly blue collar, the new membership was heavily white collar.   In effect, a new organization had been created by this autocratic individual who rubbed many people the wrong way, old and new members alike.

The aim of the resurrected association was to make arrangements for one of the top steelbands in Trinidad and Tobago, the Carib Tokyo Steel Orchestra, to perform in the Olympic Arts Festival during the 1984 Los Angeles Olympic Games.   In addition, the association was to stage, in Los Angeles, a miniature version of Carnival in Trinidad and Tobago, with Trinidadians in Los Angeles masquerading in elaborate, colorful costumes and dancing in the streets of Los Angeles

to the music of the steelband. This was just one
of many attempts on the part of the association to
implement its charter, which was to showcase the
culture of Trinidad and Tobago to the American
public. Many Afro-Trinidadians, members of the
association in particular, felt that while
Americans have been exposed to the culture of
Jamaica, to reggae music, for instance, the rich
musical and dance traditions of Trinidad and
Tobago, such as soca and steelband, have escaped
the attention of most Americans. Therefore, the
members and officers of the new association saw as
their mission the purveying of the culture of
Trinidad and Tobago, and they perceived the 1984
Olympic International Festival of Masks as the
golden opportunity to achieve their goal.

As it turned out, this venture was a success,
but not without much argument and squabbling at all
levels. I attended several planning meetings
during which there was fiery disagreement about
every step of organization, including the housing
and feeding of thirty-two "pan-men" (the steelband
musicians). These were only two of numerous major
undertakings required to make it possible for this
event to take place.

The first association mentioned above, which is
more Pan-Caribbean in orientation, does not appear
to be exempt from conflict either. Although I have
been to many of their social functions, I have not
attended organizational meetings, so I have no
personal knowledge of their operations. However,
one of the officers of this club described the
purposes, aims, and organization of the group, as
well as the dissension that seems endemic to
voluntary associations of West Indians:

> We have a club. . . I am an officer in the
> club. It's a West Indian-American club. We
> have all nationalities, all the West Indian
> islands, together with Americans. We have 60
> percent West Indians and 40 percent Americans.
> We have meetings once a month in each other's
> homes the first Friday of every month. We give

dances and shows. We give some of our money to
charity. We give donations to different
charitable institutions like Sickle Cell and
some foundations like Blue Angels. We have a
scholarship fund also. We never give money to
help (members) in case of illness or death.
It's not a good thing to do because people say
the money goes to them. Right now the club
consists of about 105 members. This is our
fourth year. Before that we were under the
name of another club. . . We existed for about
13 years, but they had disturbances and
fighting and all that, so we broke up and I
founded this one. They had too much of
fighting there. . . The problem that came up
with the other group was that one guy and his
brother wanted to be like Castro and wanted to
be president every year. They weren't giving
anybody else a chance. When we had the last
election, they were fighting to get the vote,
and a gun was fired in the crowd. So we split
up from that time on. . . Myself and four
others tried to stop them from utilizing the
money, but we never got anything. They had a
total of about $58,000 in hand, and nobody
seems to know where the money went. . . There
are about four other clubs, a Jamaican one and
a Guyanese-American one and a Trinidad club,
but I think they fell through. Many groups
fall through like that. They have a short
life.

One of the participants in the research, Bert
Diamond, recounted his attempt at forming a West
Indian association with a purpose other than simply
recreational fun, the frustrations he encountered,
and finally, his giving up:

I tried to form all types of West Indian
groups. Somehow we could never get it together
and come up with something meaningful. I don't
belong to any groups or clubs anymore.
Basically, all the associations are interested

in is giving dances. You give a dance, you
have a good time. Their basic interest is only
in giving a dance, get money, and charter a
plane to go to Trinidad for Carnival. Nothing
cultural beyond that. I wanted it to go beyond
that and really get into a cultural exchange.
It could be soccer, cricket team, or whatever,
but let's move the people between the islands.
Let's do something where we go and they come
and keep it moving. After trying
unsuccessfully for four years, I just stayed
away from it. The people themselves who are
involved, their thing is just (to have) a good
time. They don't care whether it's successful
or not, whether they make money or not: even if
they do, the money just sits in the bank
anyhow. Eventually you hear the group has
disbanded. In the 20-plus years I've been
here, I've seen many groups born and died that
way. They can't come up with any meaningful
purpose for the organization. I believe the
main problem is a lack of trust. Nobody trusts
the other person to really do something
meaningful, so they just don't want to be part
of it.

Maureen Sinclair described similar
circumstances in her experiences with a social club
to which she and Rupert once belonged:

There used to be a West Indian club back in
1973. . . To be quite honest, I can't remember
the name. It was a Trinidadian club and we
used to have meetings. For me, I have to say
that a lot of the Trinidadians bring their same
dirty habits with them. Typical bad habits,
confusion and "bacchanal". They leave and
bring them here to this big country. . . This
one say, that one say. . . always trying to
make some feud among each other and can't get
it together. This was the problem with that
club. Everyone wanted to be the boss.
Everyone was bickering with each other about

money.   They would bicker about organizing
things.   The purpose of the club was to
establish Trinidadians here. . . We both
belonged to the group but we didn't stay long.
In fact, the group broke up. We had dances and
stuff, but no scholarships. If they had kept
going and gone about it in the right way, then
it would have done something useful. One of
the points I raised was to get a Trinidadian
embassy out here. They have no representatives
here in California.   We sent a letter to
Washington, D.C. and invited one of our
representatives at the Embassy there. She came
out here and we had a function for her, but
after talking with her, you could see that she
realized that we didn't have it together. . .
You find that Trinidadians can never get to
first base because they bring their stupidity
with them from Trinidad. I feel the Jamaicans
and Guyanese and Belizeans are really
organized.

Similar sentiments were echoed by Colin Dexter,
who expressed his views on clubs and the
Trinidadian personality in this way:

I don't belong to no group.   I don't join
nothing. I been through all dat for 20 years.
A lot of Trinidadian clubs were formed and mash
up. Formed this month, mash up next month.
Meeting come. De books. He arguing about dis
and dat. Is so Trinidadians. Fighting taking
place de in people house. Trinidadians have no
national pride.   You laughin', you don't
believe that?   Because you are a social
scientist. Listen nuh, man, we Trinidadians
can't get along. We as Trinidadians is an
individual ting. Is for me to get over on you.
Dat's Trinnies. Dey call us Tricky-dadians.
That's it. We don't have no business together.
Jamaicans and Belizeans is alright. Jamaicans
come here and making it together, but anywhere
you go, a Trinnie. . . and it mash up!

Three major characteristics of West Indian voluntary associations seem to emerge from the above statements by sample members and others. The first is brevity of life span. Judging from the accounts, very few clubs live anything but a short life. With only one or two exceptions, most become defunct not long after their inception. Second, the clubs are frought with dissension and fighting. There seems to be constant feuding and bickering and people who wish to conduct themselves as dictators. This second feature seems to me to be related to the first. It would be very difficult for an organization to survive perpetual conflict. Third, the raison d'etre of the clubs appears to be for the sole purpose of partying. At least according to Bert Diamond, they lack a more meaningful purpose than this last. In fairness to the West Indian-American club described by one of its officers, this association does have a scholarship fund and makes contributions to charitable foundations, so it is not altogether bereft of civic ideals. Nevertheless, the greater part of its social agenda appears to consist of dances.

Fourth, in my opinion, the failure of these associations stems, at least partially, from the discrepancy between the individual's motives for joining and the formal charters adopted by the group. Judging from the above descriptions, it seems reasonable to infer that many individuals are inclined to join for reasons of personal glory. There is a tendency for many associations to be "top-heavy," i.e., many officers but few rank-and-file members. In short, those who wish to be part of groups also wish to give orders, have others do the work and claim credit for a successful gala event without putting in the effort. From the perspective of social organization, it would seen as though individualism triumphs over collectivism.

Justus (1976) reported in her study of West Indians in Los Angeles that there were civil rights groups and groups with a strong political orientation. I have found neither, with the possible exception of an organization to which only one research participant belongs, called the Coalition of West Indian Peoples, founded by Congressman Dymally, himself an Afro-Trinidadian. This group is trying to recruit all West Indians and concerned black Americans, such as Los Angeles City Councilman Robert Farrell, to respond to the Caribbean Basin Initiative proposed by President Reagan. The aim of the organization, according to the participant, is to bring pressure on Congress to differentiate the Caribbean from Central America. For example, they object to all the money being spent on El Salvador and, instead, wish to send some of it to the Caribbean. It is hoped that by directing attention and aid to Caribbean islands that are pro-American, these nations will be disposed to remain that way and ward off unrest and possible revolution. This group would certainly be classified as one with a political orientation, but as noted earlier, only one sample member belongs to it. The others, for the most part, appear to be apolitical.

Membership in voluntary associations does not seem to be very popular. Of the entire sample, only 30 percent are members of voluntary associations at the present time, with most holding membership in the newly resurrected Trinidadian club. One or two belong to the West Indian-American club. Of the remaining 70 percent, another 30 percent are former members of organized groups who gave up their membership for the sorts of reasons reported above by Colin Dexter, Bert Diamond, and Maureen Sinclair. The other 40 percent have never been members of organized groups and have little desire to do so.

It can be said, then, that voluntary associations do not constitute a very important part of the social life of Afro-Trinidadians in Los Angeles. There is certainly nothing resembling the numerous and diverse voluntary associations reported by Little (1957) for West African cities. West Indian voluntary associations in Los Angeles are not only few in number, they appear to be mainly of one type, namely, recreational. To my knowledge, there are no occupational, religious, or political associations among Afro-Trinidadians in Los Angeles, with the one exception noted above. I know of only one Guyanese political association, which is now either defunct or dormant. The aims of the few associations that do exist deviate quite dramatically from the mutual aid societies described by Little (1957). I know of no Afro-Trinidadian or West Indian organized groups whose purpose it is to provide members with mutual aid, support, sympathy and financial assistance in case of unemployment or illness, or funeral assistance in case of death. These types of support appear to be obtainable only at the level of kin, and possibly from close friends. Social organization among Afro-Trinidadians in Los Angeles seems to operate at the level of kinship and friendship networks but not at the level of organized groups, as very few exist. Attempts at organizing on the group level have not been very successful. Both friendship networks and voluntary associations are founded on "home-boy" ties as their guiding principle. It would appear, then, that the social worlds of Afro-Trinidadians, and West Indians generally, are very insular in structure.

CHAPTER VIII

CONCLUSIONS AND ASSESSMENT OF CARIBBEAN MIGRATION

At the beginning of this book, I tried to situate West Indian migration in its historical context, noting that in the Commonwealth Caribbean alone, a tradition of circulating populations has been going on for over 150 years (Marshall 1982). The political economy of the Caribbean has played a major role in this tradition by exerting pressures for population movement both overseas and internally, with unemployment and underemployment being key problems of the dependent economies in the region (Beckford 1972; Cross 1979; Dominguez & Dominguez 1981; Girvan 1975; Leavitt & Best 1975).

However, twentieth-century immigration policies in countries receiving immigrants have played no small part in shaping the course of this migration stream--first to North America, then to Great Britain, and back again to North America (Keely & Elwell 1981). The social structure of West Indian societies, based on clear-cut social class distinctions, has placed tremendous institutional constraints on social mobility, particularly in the domain of education, a critical institution for upward mobility (Braithwaite 1975; Lowenthal 1972; Rubin & Zavalloni 1969). Given such formidable obstacles, West Indians have often felt obliged to emigrate to expand their life options.

For example, in examining the motives that
brought participants in the research to this
country, I found self advancement to be paramount.
They came to further their education, to change
careers, to learn a trade, and to find employment.
Kinship and friendship networks between country of
origin and country of destination have made the
attainment of these goals possible.

In other words, the chain migration process
which participants in this research have used to
migrate to the United States is contingent upon the
activation of primary social relationships, namely
kinship and friendship. Sponsorship by kinsmen in
the receiving country is indispensable to potential
migrants. Kinsmen are also vital for mediating the
actual transfer and the initial settlement. Most
importantly, kinsmen are fundamental to the
adaptation of migrants transplanted to a strange
land. They assist in the adaptation process by
simultaneously keeping alive long-standing cultural
traditions and by providing a foundation from which
migrants may be socialized into new and different
patterns of behavior (Laguerre 1984).

Among members of the sample, there is strong
evidence to support the importance and vitality of
kin-based relations in their everyday lives. For
example, I found kin networks composed of a variety
of kin so extensive as to embrace more than three
generations. This is not to say that households
are multigenerational; indeed, they are not. The
most common co-residential unit is the conjugal
family, consisting of ego, spouse, and dependent
children. Nevertheless, wide-ranging and
continuous cooperation in domestic activities takes
place across co-residential units. Many essential
services are exchanged by kin across household
boundaries, such as finding housing, finding jobs,
providing transportation, and most importantly,
providing childcare. This last type of exchange is
practiced by half the participants. Another very
important service provided by 73 percent of the
sample is sharing their home with kin on an
indefinite basis. In return, kin who are guests

are expected to contribute towards rent and groceries. Apart from these economic transactions, there is also reciprocal socializing for the sake of pleasure and companionship. Chatting on the telephone and visiting each other at home occur with great frequency, usually more than once a week. Festivities like family banquets and dancing parties take place less often, usually on special occasions.

Another level of adjustment to social life in a new country occurs at the level of friendship. In contrast to having little choice in the matter of one's kin, one is able to choose one's friends. Because of its voluntary nature, friendship is significant in providing the potential for widening the scope of one's associations. In the context of international migration, friendships can facilitate the integration of immigrants into the receiving society via potential links between immigrants and non-immigrants. Of course, such potential is not always actualized, the participants in the research being a case in point.

Members of the sample engage in regular social interaction with a network of close friends in Los Angeles. However, very few of these friends are Euro-Americans. In my assessment of the range of activity fields from which intimate friends are drawn, neighbors comprise the least important source (only 1 percent). Relationships with neighbors are, at best, fleeting and superficial. A few (4 percent) of their intimate friends are recruited from the sports context, this being particularly true of the male participants. Afro-Trinidadian relations with those in the work context also tend to be superficial for the most part. Work associates comprise only 10 percent of the close friends of sample members. The majority of their intimate friends (77 percent) are introduced to them by other friends: in other words, they are friends of friends. Many of these are fellow-immigrants from Trinidad and Tobago. Others also derive from the homeland: for example, former schoolmates and family friends of long duration, although the latter do not make up a large part of their close friendship networks. However, it is worth emphasizing that the two activity fields that might provide the greatest exposure to American social life for members of the sample, neighbors and work associates, are the least significant sources of their intimate friends. Preference seems to lean towards others from the homeland.

Indeed, in terms of the ethnic and racial composition of their friendship networks in Los Angeles, by far the largest proportion (almost half) consists of fellow islanders: fellow West Indians from other Caribbean nations make up about one-third and black Americans about one-fifth. Only a tiny fraction of these networks of close friends is composed of white Americans, Latinos and Asians. In other words, the friendship networks of the participants show only slight variation in ethnicity. Fellow-islanders of the same race and culture rank highest as close friends. Fellow West Indians who are of the same race and similar culture rank second, and black Americans, who are of the same race but culturally different, rank third.

It would appear, then, that race is an important consideration in the formation of friendships. The experience of migrating to the United States has generated in sample members a heightened racial consciousness. Most of them admitted that until they came to the United States, they had never before experienced the virulent and intense racism that permeates their daily lives in the contexts of work, housing, school, and above all, the police. The racist nature of American society does not permit them to lose consciousness of their blackness. Therefore, the combined effects of black consciousness and the striking up of friendships with black Americans in the contexts of school and work, favors the evolution of a group identity based on race.

In effect, Afro-Trinidadian immigrants in Los Angeles are encapsulated in social worlds based on

cultural and racial likeness. At the level of
organized groups, even the few West Indian
voluntary associations that exist in Los Angeles
are founded on "home-fellow" ties as their guiding
principle. In contrast to the charters of other
immigrant associations, the aims of these clubs
appear to be solely recreational, their social
agendas consisting exclusively of dances and
parties. The types of associations that have been
reported for many other immigrant groups have
included mutual aid societies, conceived for the
purpose of providing financial aid, sympathy,
support, and assistance in the event of illness or
death. Among Afro-Trinidadians in Los Angeles,
however, it would appear that these types of
support are forthcoming only at the level of
kinship and friendship networks, not at the level
of organized groups. This is yet another level of
adjustment to social life in the United States.
Given the scarcity of corporate groups and the
absence of community support that might be obtained
from them, the cultivation of interpersonal ties in
the form of kinship and friendship networks becomes
critical for survival.

WEST INDIAN MIGRATION AS THE CONSTRUCTION OF
MULTIPLE OPTIONS

In accounting for their migration and the
structure of group life that I found among
Afro-Trinidadians in Los Angeles, I have drawn
inspiration from the work of Caribbean scholars who
are also concerned with West Indian migration. One
such lucid explanation of the phenomenon is social-
psychological and is based on the notion of
"strategic flexibility" (Carnegie 1982). This
flexibility is of a two-dimensional order. First,
in occupational terms, it is imperative to
construct many options. A cardinal rule of West
Indian life is never put all of one's eggs in a

single livelihood basket. Its corollaries: always
seek out multiple sources of income; always be
alert to seize whatever new training opportunities
might come one's way (Carnegie 1982:10-13, 54).
Woe betide the overspecialist!

Indeed, not so long ago, Lambros Comitas (1973)
observed among West Indians at home, a proclivity
towards "occupational multiplicity." Limited
employment opportunities being one of the realities
of West Indian life, especially at the lower end of
the economic scale, occupational pluralism is a
necessary strategy of survival. Whereas full-time
specialization in a single economic activity does
not provide an adequate livelihood, "occupational
multiplicity" offers maximal security with minimal
risk (Comitas 1973:157-173). Hence, the pursuit of
more than one occupation simultaneously in order to
survive has been a tradition of some historical
depth. In my view, migration would certainly not
extinguish this behavior. Rather, it would more
likely add more dimensions to an individual's
livelihood repertoire. In this sense, then, West
Indian migrants, being non-sedentary people, might
be considered roving practitioners of occupational
pluralism, who perceive migration as a means of
livelihood (Richardson 1983:171-182).

Put in an ecological idiom, migration
represents for many West Indians, a type of "niche
expansion" (Richardson 1983:180). But migration
requires much of the individual. In contrast to
corporate expansion which is generally accompanied
by a formal, complex system of organization,
individual livelihood expansion demands individual
energy. The result is that the necessary
organizational complexity is located within the
individual rather than a group (Richardson
1983:180). The exploitation of a livelihood niche
premised on mobility has produced personalities
extreme in two characteristics: flexibility and
individualism (Richardson 1983:181). While
flexibility in the sense of underspecialization and
being receptive to perpetual change may be

adaptive, extreme individualism may be a handicap
and exacts a high price.

For instance, in the Caribbean itself, it is
precisely this sort of individualism that has
engendered the political parochialism responsible
for the demise of the West Indies Federation
(Richardson 1983). Large-scale organizations like
the Caribbean Free Trade Association (CARIFTA) have
also fallen apart for similar reasons. Island-
nation parochialism is not confined to the region,
but is exported as well, fragmenting overseas West
Indian "communities" into segments dissociated from
each other (Henry 1982). Individualism has also
infected personal levels of social organization.
Apart from weak community organization in the
region, there is also a lack of cohesive corporate
groups. These traits have also been transplanted
to America. West Indian voluntary associations in
Los Angeles are very few in number. The few in
existence live a short life. They are fraught with
dissension. There is constant bickering: extreme
individualism promotes dictatorial behavior.
Participants in the research voiced these problems
themselves:

> We Trinidadians can't get along. We as
> Trinidadians is an individual ting.......
>
> I believe the main problem is a lack of
> trust....
>
> This was the problem with that club. Everyone
> wanted to be boss.... They would bicker about
> organizing things.

Thus, attempts at formal organization on the
group level have, more often than not, met with
failure. The price to be paid for this
individualism, then, is the need to rely on
interpersonal relationships, particularly with
close kin and trusted intimate friends. Given the
situation above, the relationship between migration
and social networks becomes quite clear. Social

networks form the microstructures of migration,
which is partly a process of building
person-to-person ties (Portes & Walton 1981:59-65).

In fact, this is the second dimension of the
concept of strategic flexibility used by Carnegie
(1982) to account for the migratory behavior of
West Indians: flexibility of interpersonal
relations which is the pattern for West Indian
migrant social organization. Social networks are
by nature fluid, protean, and capable of being
modified in form and content to meet the exigencies
of capricious circumstance. When utilized as a
survival strategy, no individual is exempt from
incorporation into this system of social relations
(Carnegie 1982). Kin who reside in receiving
countries, for example, are routinely called upon
to be sponsors of potential migrants. If no kin
are present in the receiving country, another
recourse is to obtain a "tourist" (visitor) visa,
then seek out a United States citizen to marry.
Although this plan presumes the cooperation of the
United States citizen, it confers, if successful,
permanent resident status on the former tourist and
legalizes his/her immigrant status. Not empowered
to sponsor migration, friends are called upon to
facilitate transplantation and settlement. Put
differently, strategic flexibility implies that one
should be prepared to make important personal
choices in the same way that one ought to be ready
to grasp economic opportunities that flash by.

THE ROLE OF TRANSNATIONAL SOCIAL NETWORKS IN THE
BUILDING OF CHOICES

My original purpose in studying informal social
organization among black immigrants from Trinidad
in Los Angeles was to make generalizations about
the structure of immigrant group life. In the
course of analyzing their kinship and friendship
networks, however, I discovered that the

connections of the sample members were not constrained by geography. Their primary social relations are not only transcontinental, but also multinational. These findings pose a challenge to static conceptualizations of international migration as a permanent, unidirectional process from one country to another. In previous centuries, and even in the early part of the twentieth century, this might have been an accurate assessment of transnational and intercontinental population movements. With the advent of the post-industrial age, however, latter-day migration has acquired a more dynamic character. Today, "international shuttling" is commonplace. The organizational substrate giving rise to such practices is transnational social networks.

The existence of international linkages in the form of transnational social networks has yet another implication. It invites critical re-appraisal of analytical frameworks in the social sciences founded on the dichotomous thinking of the venerable pioneers of these disciplines. This style of reasoning is adequately illustrated by the well-known rural-urban dichotomy (Redfield 1947). As identified by Ross and Weisner (1977), the logical flaw in this schema lies in conceptualizing the rural and the urban as independent social fields, as discrete social systems with antagonistic principles of organization. More accurately, the city and the country are linked in a common social field (Ross & Weisner 1977:360). In their study of rural-urban migrant networks in Kenya, Ross and Weisner (1977:359-375) proposed a superior model of the rural-urban relation based on the concept of interdependence. In the international arena, I have adopted a similar mode of analysis because I believe it does more justice to the empirical realities of the West Indian migration situation.

In my view, the concept of interdependence is a seminal one, offering illuminating insights into the dynamics of post-industrial transnational migration. Rather than perceiving immigration as strictly a national domestic problem, as do acculturation, assimilation, urbanization, and modernization theories, the notion of interdependence recognizes that sending countries and receiving countries are inextricably linked. Particularly in the study of the New Immigration (post-1965) to the United States, the idea of interdependence acknowledges that neither context may be fully understood independent of the other due to political, economic, cultural, and social ties. I will not dwell here on the political and economic linkages, as they have been lucidly analyzed by those better-versed on the subject of labor migration on a global scale (Petras 1981; Portes & Walton 1981; Sassen-Koob 1981).

With respect to cultural interdependence, more precisely between the Caribbean and the United States, there is growing cultural imperialism in the form of Americanization. Indeed, Orlando Patterson (1978) attributes the West Indian penchant for emigration to the Americanization of Afro-Caribbean societies. One feature of this Americanization is the powerful American international media network which is increasingly available to even the most remote segments of the West Indian population. American audio-visual media profoundly influence the psyches of West Indians, as well as their everyday lives (Patterson 1978). People in the Caribbean are exposed to standards of affluence, extravagant levels of consumption, and material comfort never before imagined and clearly beyond the reach of the majority. In addition, media images are reinforced by "the real thing," learned through visits and other forms of communication between America and its, geographically-speaking, Caribbean "backyard." All of this is made possible by post-industrial high-technology like jet travel and electronic marvels like the international telephone and satellite communication.

On the psychological level, Americanization has further strengthened the traditional "outward-looking" mentality which is prevalent in the West

Indies. Throughout colonial history and even today
in the neo-colonial era, the firm conviction
persists that all things imported are superior, and
all things local are inferior. The belief that
individual salvation lies abroad logically follows.
It was these sorts of considerations that led
Patterson to the inescapable inference that West
Indian migration has become institutionalized and
is indispensable for both individual and societal
survival (Patterson 1978:125).

A recent example of Americanization and the
role of the media was revealed to me by one of the
sample members. In the course of a telephone
conversation, he informed me there is now a
thriving "porno-flick on television" business in
Trinidad and Tobago. A few enterprising
individuals are selling videocassette recorders and
videotapes of pornography for a handsome profit.
They are acquiring these videotapes by flying to
Miami where they stay with friends, videotape
television programs from the cable channels in
these homes, and then take them back to Trinidad
and Tobago. It has become quite fashionable to
throw parties where "porno-flicks" are shown as the
major attraction. Another example involves a
different participant in the research who, when he
discovered herpes to be a health problem in
Trinidad and Tobago, interpreted it this way:

"Trinidadians are not going to miss out on
anything America has to offer, not even
herpes!"

Socio-economic interdependence between the
United States and Trinidad and Tobago is nourished
by Afro-Trinidadian migrants who wish to make the
most of the resources in both places by
strengthening relations in one setting to improve
life in the other. Patterns of reciprocity and the
content of reciprocity of transnational kin-based
networks show clearly that interaction with one's
intimates does not cease with the crossing of
national boundaries. Eighty percent of the

participants write letters to close kin in Trinidad and Tobago: 27 percent write as often as once a month. Ninety-three percent make international telephone calls to their close kin in Trinidad and Tobago: 50 percent do so once a month. Twenty-three percent continue to own property in Trinidad and Tobago, and 3 percent hire kin to manage property. Forty percent of the sample send remittances to their mothers who live in various parts of the Caribbean. Thirty-three percent of the sample have sent their children to the West Indies to live with close kin. According to Laguerre (1984), sending remittances and sending children home to live with relatives are two major types of persisting ties that continue to bind West Indian migrants with their homelands.

The most effective means of keeping alive network ties between participants and their loved ones in the homeland are the reciprocal patterns of regular visiting. It might even be said that they practice "international shuttling." All of the sample members take part in international visiting. Twenty percent do so as often as once a year or even more frequently. Those who used to live in New York reported that when they lived on the East coast they would visit far more often. Some go back to attend weddings and funerals and other life crises, such as illness. The two most popular occasions for visiting, however, are Christmas and Carnival. Carnival is the more spectacular of the two. Because it is an extravaganza to be rivaled only by Carnival in Brazil, Carnival in Trinidad and Tobago is the most stirring event of the annual social calendar and is something to behold. Few Trinidadians overseas can resist the temptation to participate in the frenzied revelry. More than half the sample return for Carnival: 20 percent do so every year. They do so not simply because they regard the bacchanalia as good for their mental health, but also because it is a festive time to enjoy the company of their families and friends. They can take pleasure in being face-to-face with close relatives. They can spend leisurely time "liming" (hanging out) with friends of long acquaintance, "ole-talking," drinking and partying, and catching up with what has been going on in each other's lives since they last saw one another. Participants complain that they seldom get to enjoy this unhurried style of interaction in the United States.

Apart from these international linkages, sample members also maintain transcontinental ties with close kin and friends living in New York, New Jersey, Connecticut, Boston, Miami, Houston, San Francisco, Montreal, Toronto, Calgary, Vancouver, and Washington, D.C. The patterns of reciprocity and interaction which sustain these bonds are similar in content to those just discussed in the context of transnational networks, including letters, long distance telephone calls, remittances, and child support, as well as sending children to live with relatives in other cities in North America. Patterns of reciprocal visiting also support these relationships.

The important point in this discussion is that the preservation of these ties with their social intimates in the West Indies and other cities in North America, implies personal acts of choice on the part of the sample members -- first, in the selection of particular kin and friends with whom they wish to pursue relations, and second, in the concerted effort required to sustain these connections across time and geography. It seems to me very unlikely that they would go to the trouble of retaining these elaborate, far-flung networks merely for the sake of fellowship. Although it may be possible to argue that letters and telephone calls across continents and oceans is sociability for its own sake, I nevertheless contend that the other patterns of reciprocity delineated above are not amenable to such interpretation. I construe the ownership of property in the West Indies, hiring kin to manage said property, sending remittances, sending children to live with kin, and patterns of regular visiting to be socio-economic strategies designed to anticipate times of need and to provide insurance for future uncertainties: if things do not work out in one setting, they will be able to carry on with life in another.

NON-ASSIMILATION IN AMERICAN LIFE

The fact that the primary social relationships of the Afro-Trinidadian sample criss-cross oceans and continents has considerable bearing on the question of "the absorption of immigrants." As discussed at length in Chapter I, the problem of assimilation has occupied the minds of scholars of United States immigration since the early part of the twentieth century. Assimilation in the sense of immigrant incorporation into the culture and social structure of receiving societies was viewed as not only desirable, but essential to the smooth operation of nation-states which were made up of a motley assortment of peoples from all corners of the globe. As such, assimilation was posited to be the culminating phase in the process of immigrant adjustment to the new homeland. The central thesis of this work has been that the assimilation of non-white immigrants in the United States is structurally undesirable. In the particular case of Afro-Trinidadian immigrants, there are serious impediments to their integration in American society in terms of the criteria proposed by Gordon (1964) and detailed below.

Quite apart from their importance in individual and quasi-group survival, the transnational social networks of the Afro-Trinidadian sample play a pivotal role in impeding "structural assimilation" which, in Gordon's estimation, is the "keystone of the arch of assimilation" (Gordon 1964:81). Defined as the "large-scale entrance into cliques, clubs and institutions of the host society, on the primary group level" (Gordon 1964:71), "structural assimilation," in my view, is obstructed by the transnational social networks, as well as by the

insularity of Afro-Trinidadians within the United
States. It will be recalled from preceding
chapters that the social interaction of the sample
members in Los Angeles on the primary group level
is limited almost exclusively to fellow islanders,
fellow West Indians, and black Americans. This is
also true of their social interaction in
transcontinental networks with intimates in other
cities of North America. In their transnational
networks, primary group contact is restricted even
further to fellow islanders and other West Indians.

The intimate zone of the social networks of the
participants in this research is composed of close
kin and intimate friends. Quite naturally, kin
tend to be fellow-nationals for the most part
(except where individuals have been exogamous, in
which case their affines would not be of the same
nationality). However, given the marriage patterns
of the sample (see Table 7), affines would still
tend to fall within the purview of fellow-
nationals, fellow-West Indians or Afro-Americans.
It then follows that social interaction with kin,
in whatever geographical location, would also be
confined mainly to these categories of persons. By
their own choosing, the friendship networks in Los
Angeles of the sample members are similarly
composed in ethnic and racial terms (see Table 14).
Social interaction with friends in Los Angeles,
then, would take on the same componential
boundaries. It would appear that members of the
sample associate with members of the "core society"
on the level of secondary group contacts, that is
to say, on the job, in school, or in impersonal
public settings.

It may be inferred from the above that the
"structural assimilation" of Afro-Trinidadian
immigrants in the United States has not come about.
Rather, the situation that obtains is one of
"structural pluralism" (Gordon 1964:159). With
respect to non-white populations in the United
States, it might be said that their American
experience is one of structurally separate
networks, cliques, associations, and institutions.

In short, non-white immigrants live in bounded communities or subsocieties which enable them to have only secondary, superficial contact with those outside (Gordon 1964:234-235). The primacy of "structural assimilation" in the assimilation paradigm lies in the theorem that the process of immigrant absorption hinges on social structural participation, not simply on the adoption of new values, attitudes, and behavior; in other words, not only on acculturation (Gordon 1964:67). Once this critical phase has been accomplished, all other phases inevitably follow (Gordon 1964:81). Indeed, structural assimilation paves the way for "marital assimilation" or large-scale intermarriage, another stage essential to completing the process (Gordon 1964:80).

A cursory examination of the marriage patterns of the sample members (see Table 7) demonstrates that conjugal partners are chosen largely from the same social categories as those just discussed in relation to kin and friends. It is readily apparent that marital assimilation into the "core society" is not a reality for the participants in the research. Of the 97 percent who are married, 70 percent are married to Afro-Trinidadians, 17 percent to Afro-Americans, and 7 percent to Afro-Jamaicans. Only one individual was married to an Anglo-American, and it is worth noting that this marriage ended in divorce after three years. Simply stated, intermarriage with majority members of American society is a rare phenomenon among Afro-Trinidadians, and as such, is unlikely to take place on a large scale.

What is far more likely, and indeed has already been documented, is the absorption of West Indians into the structurally separate black American subsociety. Laguerre (1984) has suggested that this is true of the Haitian experience in America as well. In sum, if assimilation can be said to have taken place at all, it must be of a different variety altogether. Rather than a status change from immigrant to American, as posited by assimilationists, what we may observe in the case of black immigrants is a change from stranger to minority.

All these things considered, it might be suggested that the immigration of racially distinct people into American society ought not to be analyzed independently of the problem of racial minorities in this country. The social integration of the New Immigrants on a large scale is essentially undesirable except, perhaps, from an economic point of view. Portes (1981:285) has argued, for example, that immigrant labor in the peripheral sectors of the economy, i.e., in the secondary labor market, serves a valuable function in disciplining the domestic labor force. Apart from their possible structural incorporation in the secondary sector and/or in the "immigrant enclave" sector, heterogeneous enterprises organized in immigrant concentrations to serve distinct immigrant markets (Portes 1981:290-295), black immigrants have been effectively excluded from full participation in American group life.

Barriers to assimilation assume the form of racial restrictions built into the structure of the major institutions of America (Blauner 1972), such as housing, employment, education, public services, and political rights. Residential segregation has been the sine qua non of maintaining, if not widening, the social gulf that separates blacks and whites in America. In a recent survey of racial segregation in housing (Hirschman 1983:407; Massey 1981:68), it was noted that there has been little or no decline in the level of residential segregation between blacks and whites in urban areas throughout the country, and social class differences cannot account for the high rates of segregation. Examination of the residential locations of the sample members in Los Angeles showed the following patterns: 63 percent live in exclusively black areas; 17 percent live in racially-mixed (integrated) districts; while 20 percent live in predominantly white neighborhoods. These patterns of residence seem to bear no strong relationship to the occupations of the sample

members. Professionals, as well as working-class
individuals, are found in each category, confirming
general patterns of residential segregation.
Participants in the research have also been
subjected to discrimination in employment and
education. Half of the sample members recounted
incidents of racial discrimination at work, and for
those who furthered their education in the United
States, such incidents took place at school. These
accounts were volunteered by those in occupations
of high and low prestige alike, ranging from
doctors and managers to electricians and auto
mechanics. Rather than declining in prominence,
race continues to be of enduring significance in
America (Oliver 1980).

Coming from societies in which social class
distinctions often dwarfed racial considerations,
the participants in the research have entered a
two-tiered racial system that pits whites against
blacks. Their post-migration experiences,
therefore, have served to underscore their racial
consciousness, although several admitted racial
ambivalence, particularly occurring when they first
arrived in the United States. Other scholars have
also reported racial ambivalence among Caribbean
immigrants in America (Coombs 1970; Dominguez 1975;
Foner 1978). They suggest that black West Indians
reject a complete identification with blackness, on
the one hand, because they fear the concomitant
stigma and are reluctant to jeopardize their
aspirations towards middle-class status; on the
other hand, they have great empathy for black
Americans, having personally suffered similar
injustices. They thus tread a tightrope between
these two positions.

Laguerre (1984) goes so far as to propose that
Haitians, in their adaptation to life in America,
engage in a certain duplicity to manipulate
ethnicity to their advantage. He claims, for
instance, that in interactions with whites, West
Indians assume West Indian identities to emphasize
their "foreign-ness," and when running for
political office, they identify themselves as

blacks (Laguerre 1984:157). I suggest that the resolution of this internal conflict leans toward a group identity based on race. "Identificational assimilation," defined as "the development of a sense of peoplehood based exclusively on the host society" (Gordon 1964:71), has not appeared on the West Indian immigrant scene. Instead, what has evolved over time among West Indians with exposure to American traditions, is a black consciousness, shaped by their daily encounters with racism and nourished by their friendships formed with black Americans. In light of these developments, I would submit that race is gaining salience in the lives of black immigrants to the United States as a principle of collective identity and potential political action.

Although there is great potential for group formation based on blackness at the present time, such a movement among West Indians in Los Angeles is only in a germinating phase. My research has shown that organized groups of West Indians in Los Angeles are few and tend to be short-lived. The lack of mature, well-developed voluntary organizations in the West Indian "community" in Los Angeles is thus the major stumbling block towards unity in action. But the very existence of a group called the Coalition of West Indian Peoples founded by Congressman Dymally, himself an Afro-Trinidadian who has been inspired to take an active part in United States national politics, should be interpreted as a sign that the West Indian collectivity is moving in that direction.

For it is precisely in the arena of politics that the migration of black West Indians embodies high hopes for altering the balance of power in the United States. Above all else, the New Immigration has transformed the size and shape of ethnic America by re-arranging the racial composition of its population. In the special case of Caribbean immigration, its major impact has been to expand the size of the black population in the United States. There is potential power in numbers. A conservative estimate of the Caribbean presence in

America lies in the vicinity of four million. This figure includes migrants from the English-speaking, Dutch-speaking, French-speaking, and Spanish-speaking Carib@bean. Given the constancy of racism, the persistance of discrimination, and the tenacity of racial-political conflict, as well as their corollaries, the persistence of prejudice, the continuation of discrimination and the need for "civic assimilation" (Gordon 1964:71), the addition of the Caribbean presence to the political landscape should enhance the political voice of blacks in America.

THE BEST OF BOTH WORLDS

This odyssey through the personal lives of the participants in the research has revealed that migration for them has been a quest for the best of both worlds, for the freedom to choose between more than one life option. They have actualized this goal by keeping one foot in the Caribbean with the other foot in America. For them, America symbolizes a wealth of material options. They all left Trinidad and Tobago at a point in their lives when they were in a state of stagnation. They believed that in America they could acquire skills if they had none. Those who already had skills believed they could acquire additional ones. Those who were unemployed believed they could not only get jobs, but better-paying and more prestigious ones. And with these well-paying jobs, they could have all manner of material comforts. For most of the participants, these dreams have come to fruition.

But in the midst of the abundance many have achieved in America, what they all miss most are things of the spirit: the Trinidadian sensibility in food, music, and Carnival and the Trinidadian style of interpersonal relationships, especially joking. In short, they pine for their Trinidadian

souls. And so they shuttle back and forth between
the two worlds, because they have passed their
auspicious moment of return migration.   As one
participant put it:

> They can't live in Trinidad because there's so
> much opportunity out here, like to do things,
> work and make a decent living, that if they
> went home they would be really lost.   I find
> with them, they want to be home but yet they
> can't be home.   You know this kinda thing?

For most, then, there seems little choice but
to keep up their Caribbean connections while
remaining in America: to return periodically for
spiritual revitalization while accepting the best
America has to offer.

NOTES

CHAPTER 4

1. Susu is a form of rotating credit association.
    Ivan Light (1972:30-32) discusses the
    institution of esusu, of Yoruba origin, among
    West Indians in the United States which seems
    to have been transplanted to the West Indies
    but not to the United States. This form of
    rotating credit is called susu in Trinidad,
    pardners in Jamaica, meeting in Barbados and
    box money in Guyana. It is based on the
    principle of pooling funds and rotating the pot
    among members. Light (1972:19-44) argues this
    institution favors entrepreneurial behavior
    among West Indians in contrast to black
    Americans.

CHAPTER 5

2. Ivan Light (1972:33) argues that in contrast to
    black Americans, West Indians show a
    "remarkable propensity to operate small
    enterprises." His explanation is based, in
    part, on West Indian retention of an African
    institution, the rotating credit association,
    not found among black Americans. More
    importantly, Light (1972:170-190) suggests

189

that as far as social organization is concerned, West Indians, like Japanese and Chinese immigrants, have better organized communities, i.e., have viable voluntary associations, among other things, whereas black Americans exhibit much individualism. My findings show a lack of enterprise on the part of Afro-Trinidadians in Los Angeles.

CHAPTER 7

3. St. Clair is an upper-class district of the capital city of Port-of-Spain, Trinidad. The area consists of castle-like mansions in which the plantocracy once resided, the mansions being surrounded by formal gardens and extensive grounds.

4. John-John is a slum on the outskirts of Port of Spain, the capital city of Trinidad. It is made up of delapidated shacks built on steep hillsides much in the same manner as the favelas of Brazilian cities.

5. New York is used in this instance by the Mighty Sparrow as a generic term to refer to the United States as a whole, since New York is the region of the United States in which most West Indians reside. Indeed, during my return visits to Trinidad, most people I encounter assume that I live in New York when they find out that I live in America. Most Trinidadians have no conception of the geographical distance separating Los Angeles from New York. The only meaning Los Angeles has for them is as the home of the "movie stars."

6. In his comparative study of enterprising
    behavior among Japanese and Chinese immigrants
    and black Americans, Ivan Light (1972:170-190)
    drew attention to the pivotal role played by
    community organization, particularly a strong
    sense of collective orientation and stable
    voluntary associations, in promoting the
    establishment of small businesses among
    Japanese and Chinese immigrants. In contrast,
    small businesses were rare among black
    Americans. Light (1972) attributed this black
    American behavior to their strong sense of
    individualism and their weak sense of ethnic
    identity. Among West Indians, he found much
    ethnic enterprise and inferred from this
    strong community organization on their part.
    My findings run directly counter to those of
    Light (1972). Indeed, among Afro-Trinidadians,
    I found extreme individualism coupled with an
    inability to organize on the group level.

INITIAL INTERVIEW SCHEDULE

The following questions were put to the participants in the research on an informal basis. No exact phrasing or strict sequencing of questions was used. Variants of the questions that appear below were inserted at appropriate moments in the conversation to elicit the desired information. The initial interview was intended to extract only general types of information in the following categories: personal migration history, including length of residence in various parts of the world; motives for migration; and age, place of birth, occupation, education and employment history.

MIGRATION HISTORY

1. Where were you born?
2. When were you born?
3. When did you leave the West Indies?
4. What made you decide to come to the United States?
5. Did you manage this move on your own or did you have help from relatives or friends?
6. Did you live anywhere else between coming to the States and leaving the West Indies?

7. How long did you live there?
8. Where else in the States besides L.A. have you
    lived?
9. How long did you live there?
10. What brought you to Los Angeles?
11. How long have you been living in Los Angeles?

OCCUPATION

1. What kind of work did you do back home?
2. What kind of work do you do in Los Angeles?
3. Where do you work?
4. How long have you worked there?
5. Did you find this job on your own or did you
    have help from relatives, or friends or
    agencies?
6. What other kinds of work have you done?   (In
    L.A. and elsewhere.)
7. Are you happy with your job now or would you
    like to change?
8. Ideally, what kind of work would you like to
    do?
9. Have you had trouble finding work?
10. Have you had trouble holding down a job?

EDUCATION

1. How far did you go in school back home?
2. Have you continued your schooling since coming
    to the States?
3. What type of training have you received?
4. How long did you train?
5. Did you finish the course and receive a diploma
    or certificate?

APPENDIX B

SECOND INTERVIEW SCHEDULE

A second interview was conducted at the home of the participants. It was semi-structured to elicit responses to specific questions about marriage, marriage or relationship longevity, children living at home, children living elsewhere, household members besides the participant, spouse/mate and their children, and child-care arrangements. Partial genealogies were obtained for kinsmen living in Los Angeles, in other cities of North America and in various parts of the West Indies.

Also examined were the size, range and density of kin networks, as well as the frequency and the intensity of interaction, and the type of exchange taking place during interaction such as the sending of remittances and the ownership of property. Another target of investigation was the intimate zone of friendship networks. Participants were asked about their closest friends in various parts of the globe, the nature and content of those relationships and the frequency and the intensity of interaction. The size and range of friendships networks and density of network sectors were also assessed, in addition to the ethnic and racial composition of these friendship networks.

MARRIAGE AND CHILDREN

1. Are you married, divorced or single? Or living together?
2. How long have you been married? How long have you known each other?
3. How did you meet each other? Where did you meet?
4. What nationality is your mate?
5. How many children do you have? How old are they?
6. Do you have any children not living here with you? How old are they?
7. Where do they live? With whom?
8. How long have they lived there?
9. Do you keep in touch with them? How often? By what means?
10. Do you keep in touch with the mother/father of these children? How? How often?
11. Do you contribute to their support?

ORGANIZATION OF FAMILY ACTIVITIES

1. Does anyone else live in this house besides your mate and children?
2. Do they contribute to the rent or mortgage?
3. Do they contribute groceries or food money?
4. What are the main tasks to be done around the house?
5. Who cooks together? Who eats together?

CHILD CARE

1. Did you have help immediately after your child was born? From whom?
2. Who took care of the older children at that time?
3. Who is responsible for minding the children at home?
4. Who minds them when you go out?
5. Who minds them while you are at work?
6. Do you ever mind the children of your relatives and friends? How often?
7. Who is responsible for taking the children to school?
8. Who supervises their contact with other children?
9. Who makes decisions about the children?
10. Do you ever disagree about what is to be done?
11. What sorts of plans do you have for the children's schooling?
12. What would you like them to be when they grow up?
13. What do you think is the most important thing about bringing up children?

KINSMEN IN TRINIDAD AND TOBAGO AND OTHER PARTS OF THE WEST INDIES

1. How many relatives do you have living in Trinidad and the West Indies?
2. How are they related to you?
3. How often do you keep in touch with them?
4. How do you keep in touch? By phone? By letters? By visits? Special occasions?
5. Do these relatives ever come up to visit and stay with you? How often? How long?
6. Do you ever stay with them in the W.I.? Which ones? How often? For how long?

7. Do your children stay with them? How often? How long?
8. How often do you go back to the West Indies?
9. Do you own any property in Trinidad or other places in the W.I.?
10. Do you ever send money back to the W.I.? To whom? How often?

KINSMEN IN U.S.A. AND CANADA

1. How many relatives do you have living in the U.S.A. and Canada?
2. How are they related to you?
3. Where do they live?
4. How often do you keep in touch with them?
5. How do you keep in touch? By letters? By phone? Visits? Holidays? Parties?
6. Have you ever stayed with any of these relatives? How long?
7. Have they ever stayed with you in your home? How long?
8. Have they helped you with finding a job or finding a place to live?
9. Do you own any property in common with any of these relatives?
10. Are any of these relatives business partners?

KINSHIP NETWORKS

1. In case of an emergency, which of these relatives could you count on?
2. Since coming to the States, have you lived in the home of any of these relatives? For how long?
3. Have any of these relatives lived in your home in the States? For how long?

4. Which of these relatives know each other? (network density.)
5. Which of these relatives have contact with each other when you are not present? (network density).
6. Do you have close ties with persons whom you regard as relatives but who are not related to you by blood? What kind of contact do you have with them? (fictive kin.)
7. Do you exchange presents at Christmas time or birthdays or any other time? With whom?
8. How often do you go back home? How long do you stay? Who do you stay with?
9. Do you send money home? To whom? How much? How often?
10. Do you send any of your children back home for holidays or any other time? How long do they stay? With whom?

FRIENDSHIP NETWORKS

1. Can you tell me about your closest friends?
2. How many live in the W.I.? In L.A.? Elsewhere?
3. Are these close friends West Indian? If not, what nationality and race are they?
4. How many are what nationality and what race?
5. Are they in a similar line of work?
6. How did you meet them? (Sources of recruitment.)
7. How long have you known them?
8. What do they do for a living?
9. Have you ever lived in this person's home? If so, for how long?
10. Has this person ever lived in your home? If so, for how long?
11. How often do you keep in touch with this person?
12. What sort of contact do you have with this friend? Letters? Visit? Telephone?

Have dinner out with them? Go to the movies
with them? Invite them home for dinner?
Invite them to parties? Go out with them?

13. How many people from work are you friends with?
14. How long have you known them?
15. How many of them are friends with each other?
16. What sort of contact do you have with them?
    Eat lunch together? Have dinner together?
    Invite them to your home?
17. How many of your neighbors are you friends
    with?
18. How long have you known them?
19. How many of them have contact with each other?
20. What sort of contact do you have with them?
21. Are your children friends with them? If so,
    are they close friends?
22. In case of an emergency, which of your friends
    could you count on?
23. How many of your friends know each other?
    (network density.)
24. Which of your friends have contact with each
    other without you being present? (density.)

VOLUNTARY ASSOCIATIONS AND COMMUNITY INVOLVEMENT

1. Do you belong to any social group or club? If
   so, which one?
2. What is the purpose of the group?
3. Who is allowed to join?
4. How old is the group?
5. How is it organized?
6. How many people belong to this group?
7. How often does the group meet?
8. Can you tell me more about the activities of
   the group?

GENERAL

1. How is life in L.A. different from life in N.Y.?
2. What do you like or dislike about life in the U.S.A.?
3. Have you had any experiences with discrimination in this country?
4. Do you have any plans to move back to Trinidad in the future?
5. Do you think coming to the United States was a good move? Why?
6. What country do you consider to be your "home"?

TABLES

TABLE 1

Annual Average Immigration to the U.S. by Region of Origin

Region	1961 – 1965		1969 – 1976	
	Annual Average	Percent	Annual Average	Percent
Europe	122,155	42.1	92,907	24.2
Asia	21,611	7.5	116,255	30.3
Africa	2,564	0.9	6,833	1.8
Oceania	1,307	0.5	3,161	0.8
N. America	118,804	41.0	142,406	37.1
S. America	23,609	8.1	21,786	5.7
Other	13	–	2	–

Source: Keely & Elwell 1981: 189

TABLE 2

Population in the United States from
Four Caribbean Nations

Nationality	Total Number in the United States	
	1980 Census*	I.N.S. 1980 Statistics**
Barbados	21,425	14,866
Jamaica	253,268	95,468
Trinidad & Tobago	43,812	34,386
Guyana	31,853	21,728

Sources: * U.S. Census, Bureau of the Census 20th, 1980 Population, Ancestry of Population by State 1980

** U.S. Dept. of Justice, Immigration & Naturalization Service, Annual Reports 1980

TABLE 3

Gender, Place of Birth, Age and Marital Status of Sample
(N=30)

	Male	%	Female	%
Gender	15	50	15	50
Trinidad-Born	15	50	15	50
Age: 20 – 29 years	1	6.6	2	13.3
30 – 39 years	7	46.6	8	53.3
40 – 49 years	5	33.3	5	33.3
50 – 59 years	1	6.6	0	
60 – 69 years	1	6.6	0	
Marital Status				
Single	1	6.6	1	6.6
Cohabiting	1	6.6	1	6.6
Married	8	53.3	10	66.6
Divorced	5	33.3	3	20.0

TABLE 4

Educational Attainment Levels of Afro-Trinidadian Sample

(N=30)

Highest Level of Education Completed	Male	%	Female	%
Primary School	15	100	15	100
Secondary School	9	60	15	100
Technical School	7	46.6	6	40.6
Incomplete University	0	–	3	20
University (Bachelor's Degree)	8	53.3	5	33.3
Incomplete Post-Graduate	3	20	0	–
Post-Graduate University	2	13.3	0	–
Professional School	4	26.6	5	33.3

TABLE 5

Occupational Group Characteristics of Afro-Trinidadian Sample

(N=30)

Occupational Group	Male	%	Female	%
Professional/Technical	4	26.6	5	33.3
Managerial/Administrative	3	20.0	3	20.0
Clerical	1	6.7	6	40.0
Sales	1	6.7	0	-
Craftsmen	6	40.0	0	-
Students	0	-	1	6.7

TABLE 6

The Chain Migration Process

(N=30)

Migration Sponsored by Primary Relations	Male	Female	%
Sponsorship by Kin and Fictive Kin	10	9	63
Sponsorship by Friends	2	4	20
Other Sponsors of Migration			
Employer of Domestics	0	2	7
College/University	2	0	7
Independent	1	0	3

TABLE 7

Ethnic Membership of Mates of Afro-Trinidadian Sample

(N=30)

Ethnic Membership of Mate	Number of Participants	%
Afro-Trinidadian	21	70
Afro-American	5	17
Afro-Jamaican	2	7
Anglo-American	1	3
Unattached	1	3

TABLE 8

Size and Location of Kin Networks of Afro-Trinidadian Sample

(N=30)

Number of Intimate Kin	Number of Participants		
	L.A.	N.A.*	W.I.**
0	3	6	0
1 – 5	13	6	7
6 – 10	7	9	1
11 – 15	4	4	11
16 – 20	0	3	6
21 – 25	1	1	5
26 – 30	2	1	0

*Elsewhere in North America

** West Indies (Caribbean)

TABLE 9

Interactional Content of Kin Relationships in North America
(N=24)*

Type of Kin Interaction	Number of Participants	%**
Letter-writing	11	37
Once a Month	6	20
Once every 3 Months	5	17
Family Newsletter	1	3
Telephone (Long Distance)	24	80
More than Once a Week	5	17
Once a Week	5	17
Once every 2 Weeks	6	20
Once a Month	3	10
Less than Once a Month	5	17
Remittances	2	7
Own Property in Common	1	3
Child Support	2	7
Child Fostering	4	13

*Six Participants have no kin in North America
**Responses total more than 100% due to Multiple Responses

TABLE 10

Interactional Content of Kin Relationships in the West Indies

(N=30)

Type of Kin Interaction	Number of Participants	%*
Letter-writing		
Once every 2 Weeks	24	80
Once a Month	5	17
Once every 6 Months	8	27
Once every 6 Months	6	20
Once a Year	5	17
Telephone (Overseas)	28	93
Once a Month	15	50
Once every 6 Months	9	30
Once a Year	4	13
Remittances	12	40
Child Fostering by W.I. Kin	10	33
Owning Property in Common	7	23
Hire Kin to Manage Property	1	3

* Responses total more than 100% because of Multiple Responses

TABLE 11

Transcontinental and International Visiting Patterns

Transcontinental Visiting (N=24)*	Number of Participants	%**
Vacation Visits		
Once a Month	1	3
Once every 6 Months	1	3
Once a Year	10	33
Once every 2 Years	5	17
Once every 3 or 4 Years	7	24
International Visiting (N=30)		
Vacation Visits and Gifts		
More than Once a Year	1	3
Once a Year	6	20
Once every 2 Years	7	24
Once every 3 to 7 Years	15	50
Less than Once every 10 Years	1	3
Christmas	4	13
Carnival	16	53
Family Reunions	2	7
Life Crises (e.g. Funerals)	4	13

* Six Participants have no Kin in North America

** Responses total more than 100% because of Multiple Responses

TABLE 12

Size and Location of Friendship Networks of Afro-Trinidadian Sample

(N=30)

Number of Intimate Friends	Number of Participants		
	L.A.	N.A.*	W.I.**
0	0	6	4
1 – 4	4	3	14
5 – 10	15	16	12
11 – 15	7	5	0
16 – 20	2	0	0
21 – 25	2	0	0

*Elsewhere in North America

** West Indies (Caribbean)

TABLE 13

Average Sector Density of Social Networks*

(N=30)

Sector	Los Angeles	Density(%) North America	West Indies
Kinship	100.0	98.3	94.9
Work Associates	80.4	85.9	90.3
Friendship	64.5	73.5	82.6
Neighborhood	12.1	67.8	88.7

*Intimate Zone Only

215

TABLE 14

Ethnic and Racial Composition of Friendship Networks in L.A.*

(N=30)

Ethnicity and Race of Friends	% Friendship Network
Fellow-Islanders	46.0
Fellow-West Indians	29.0
American (Black)	21.0
American (White)	2.0
Latino (Puerto Rican/Mexican)	1.0
Asian (Filipino/Hawaiian)	0.5
British/Australian/Indian/Pakistani	0.5

*Intimate Zone Only

BIBLIOGRAPHY

Barnes, J.A.
    1972   "Social Networks," Addison-Wesley
                Module in Anthropology,   No. 26.
                Reading, Addison-Wesley.

Beckford, George
    1972   Persistent Poverty: Underdevelopment
                in Plantation Economies of the Third
                World. New York: Oxford University
                Press.

Blauner, Robert
    1972   Racial Oppression in America.   New
                York: Harper and Row.

Boissevain, Jeremy
    1974   Friends of Friends.   Oxford: Basil
                Blackwell.

Bott, Elizabeth
    1971 (1957)   Family and Social Network.
                Second Edition, New York: Free
                Press.

Braithwaite, Lloyd
    1975 (1953)   Social Stratification in
                Trinidad.   Mona, Jamaica:
                Institute of Social and Economic
                Research.   University of the
                West Indies.

216

Braveboy-Wagner, Jacqueline
    1983   "Current Developments in Trinidad and
              Tobago." Caribbean Studies
              Newsletter, Vol. 10(1): 17-19.

Bryce-Laporte, Roy S.
    1972   "Black Immigrants: The Experience of
              Invisibility and Inequality." Journal
              of Black Studies, Vol. 3, (1): 29-56.

    1976   "The United States Role in Caribbean
              Migration: Background to the
              Problem," In R. Bryce-Laporte & D.
              Mortimer (eds.). Caribbean
              Immigration to the United States.
              Washington, D.C.: Research Institute
              on Immigration and Ethnic Studies,
              Smithsonian Institution, Pp. 1-14.

    1977   "Visibility of the New Immigrants".
              Society, Vol. 14, (6): 18-22.

    1980   "The New Immigration: A Challenge to
              our Sociological Imagination," In R.
              Bryce-Laporte (ed.), Sourcebook on
              the New Immigration: Implications
              for the United States and the
              International Community. New Jersey:
              Transaction Books, Pp. 459-472.

Caldwell, J.C.
    1969   African Rural-Urban Migration.
              Canberra: Australia National
              University Press.

Carnegie, Charles
    1982   "Strategic Flexibility in the West
              Indies: A Social Psychology of
              Caribbean Migrations." Caribbean
              Review, Vol. 11(1): 10-13;54.

Choldin, Harvey
    1973   "Kinship Networks in the Migration
              Process." International Migration
              Review, Vol. 7(2): 163-175.

Comitas, Lambros
    1973   "Occupational Multiplicity in Rural
              Jamaica," In, L. Comitas & D.
              Lowenthal (eds.). Work and Family
              Life: West Indian Perspectives. New
              York: Anchor Books, Pp. 157-173.

Coombs, Orde
    1970   "West Indians in New York." New York
              Magazine, July, Vol. 13: 28-32.

Cornelius, Wayne
    1984   "New Immigration `Remedy' Has Long
              Record of Failure," Los Angeles
              Times, June 22, Part II, P7, Col. 1.

Cross, Malcolm
    1979   Urbanization and Urban Growth in the
              Caribbean. London: Cambridge
              University Press.

Cubitt, Tessa
    1973   "Network Density Among Urban
              Families," In J. Boissevain & J.C.
              Mitchell (eds.), Network Analysis:
              Studies in Human Interaction. The
              Hague: Mouton Publishers, Pp. 67-82.

Dominguez, Virginia R.
    1975   From Neighbor to Stranger: The
              Dilemma of Caribbean Peoples in the
              United States. New Haven: Antilles
              Research Program, Yale University.

Dominguez, Virginia and Jorge Dominguez
    1981   The Caribbean: Its Implications for
              the United States. New York: The
              Foreign Policy Association.

Eisenstadt, S.N.
    1954   The Absorption of Immigrants.
                London: Routledge, Kegan, Paul.

Epstein, A.L.
    1969   "The Network and Urban Social
                Organization," In, J.C. Mitchell
                (ed.), Social Networks in Urban
                Situations. Manchester: Manchester
                University Press, Pp. 77-116.

Foner, Nancy
    1978   Jamaica Farewell: Jamaican Migrants
                in London. Berkeley: University of
                California Press.

Geschwender, James A.
    1978   Racial Stratification in America.
                Dubuque, Iowa: William C. Brown
                Company, Publishers.

Girvan, Norman
    1975   "Caribbean Mineral Economy," In, G.
                Beckford (ed.). Caribbean Economy:
                Dependence and Backwardness.
                Kingston, Jamaica: Institute of
                Social and Economic Research,
                University of the West Indies, Pp.
                92-129.

Glazer, Nathan and Daniel P. Moynihan
    1963   Beyond the Melting Pot. Cambridge,
                Massachusetts: The M.I.T. Press.

Gordon, Milton M.
    1964   Assimilation in American Life: The
                Role of Race Religion and National
                Origins. New York: Oxford University
                Press.

Hamid, Ansley
1981   A Pre-Capitalist Mode of Production: Ganja and the Rastafarians in San Fernando, Trinidad. Unpublished Ph.D. Dissertation, Columbia University.

Hannerz, Ulf
1967   "Gossip, Networks and Culture in a Black American Ghetto." Ethnos, 1(4): 35-60.

1969   Soulside: Inquiries into Ghetto Culture and Community. New York: Columbia University Press.

Henry, Frances
1982   "A Note on Caribbean Migration to Canada." Caribbean Review, Vol. 11 (1): 38-41.

Herskovits, Melville J.
1958 (1938)   Acculturation: The Study of Culture Contact. Gloucester, Massachusetts: Peter Smith, Publisher.

Hirschman, Charles
1983   "America's Melting Pot Reconsidered," Annual Review of Sociology, Vol. 9: 397-423.

Jacobson, David
1971   "Mobility, Continuity and Urban Social Organization." Man, Vol. 6(4): 630-644.

Justus, Joyce Bennett
    1976   "West Indians in Los Angeles:
                Community and Identity," In, R.
                Bryce-Laporte & D. Mortimer (eds.),
                Caribbean Immigration to the United
                States. Washington, D.C.: Research
                Institute on Immigration and Ethnic
                Studies, Smithsonian Institution, Pp.
                130-148.

Keefe, Susan Emley
    1980   "Personal Communities in the City:
                Support Networks Among Mexican-
                Americans and Anglo-Americans" Urban
                Anthropology, Vol. 9(1): 51-74.

Keely, Charles B. and Patricia J. Elwell
    1981   "International Migration: Canada and
                the United States," In, M. Kritz, C.
                Keely & S. Tomasi (eds.), Global
                Trends in Migration: Theory and
                Research on International Population
                Movements. New York: Center for
                Migration Studies, Pp. 181-207.

Koegel, Paul
    1982   Rethinking Support Systems: A
                Qualitative Investigation into the
                Nature of Social Support.
                Unpublished Ph.D. Dissertation,
                University of California, Los
                Angeles.

Kritz, Mary
    1981   "International Migration Patterns in
                the Caribbean Basin: An Overview,"
                In, M. Kritz, C. Keely & S. Tomasi
                (eds.). Global Trends in Migration:
                Theory and Research on International
                Population Movements. New York:
                Center for Migration Studies, Pp.
                208-233.

Laguerre, Michel S.
    1984   American Odyssey: Haitians in New
              York City.   Ithaca: Cornell
              University Press.

Levitt, Kari and Lloyd Best
    1975   "Character of Caribbean Economy," In,
              G. Beckford (ed.), Caribbean Economy:
              Dependence and Backwardness.
              Kingston, Jamaica: Institute of
              Social and Economic Research,
              University of the West Indies, Pp.
              34-60.

Li, Peter S.
    1977   "Fictive Kinship, Conjugal Tie and
              Kinship Chain Among Chinese
              Immigrants in the United States."
              Journal of Comparative Family
              Studies, Vol. 8(1):   47-63.

Light, Ivan H.
    1972   Ethnic Enterprise in America.
              Berkeley: University of California
              Press.

Little, Kenneth
    1957   "The Role of Voluntary Associations
              in West African Urbanization."
              American Anthropologist, Vol. 59:
              579-596.

Litwak, Eugene and Ivan Szelenyi
    1969   "Primary Group Structures and their
              Functions: Kin, Neighbors and
              Friends." American Sociological
              Review, Vol. 34(2): 465-481.

Lowenthal, David
    1972   West Indian Societies.   New York:
              Oxford University Press.

MacDonald, John S. and Leatrice D. MacDonald
    1964   "Chain Migration, Ethnic Neighborhood
               Formation and Social Networks."
               Milbank Memorial Fund Quarterly, Vol.
               42(1): 82-97.

Marshall, Dawn
    1982   "The History of Caribbean Migrations:
               The Case of the West Indies."
               Caribbean Review, Vol. 11 (1): 6-9;
               52-53.

Massey, Douglas
    1981   "Dimensions of the New Immigration to
               the United States and the Prospects
               for Assimilation." Annual Review of
               Sociology, Vol. 7: 57-85.

Mayer, Philip
    1961   Townsmen or Tribesmen.   Cape Town:
               Oxford University Press.

McLaughlin, Megan E.
    1981   West Indian Immigrants: Their Social
               Networks and Ethnic Identification.
               Unpublished D.S.W.   Dissertation,
               Columbia University.

Metzger, L. Paul
    1971   "American Sociology and Black
               Assimilation: Conflicting
               Perspectives." American Journal of
               Sociology. Vol. 76(4): 627-647.

Midgett, Douglas K.
    1975   "West Indian Ethnicity in Great
               Britain,"   In, H. Safa & B. DuToit
               (eds.), Migration and Development.
               The Hague: Mouton Publishers, Pp. 57-
               81.

Mills, C. Wright
1959 The Sociological Imagination." New York: Oxford University Press.

Mintz, Sidney
1971 "The Caribbean as a Socio-Cultural Area," In, M. Horowitz (ed.). Peoples and cultures of the Caribbean. New York: Natural History Press, Pp. 17-46.

Mitchell, J. Clyde
1969 "The Concept and Use of Social Networks," In, J.C. Mitchell (ed.), Social Networks in Urban Situations. Manchester: Manchester University Press, Pp. 1-50.

1974 "Social Networks." Annual Review of Anthropology, Vol. 3: 274-299.

Oliver, Melvin L.
1980 "The Enduring Significance of Race." Journal of Ethnic Studies, Vol. 7(4): 79-91.

Palmer, Ransford W.
1974 "A Decade of West Indian Migration to the United States, 1962-1972: An Economic Analysis." Social and Economic Studies, Vol. 23: 571-588.

Park, Robert E.
1950 Race and Culture. Glencoe, Illinois: The Free Press.

Park, Robert E. and Ernest W. Burgess
1924 Introduction to the Science of Sociology. Chicago: University of Chicago Press.

Patterson, Orlando
1975   "Context and Choice in Ethnic
            Allegiance: A Theoretical Framework
            and Caribbean Case Study" In, N.
            Glazer & D. Moynihan (eds.),
            Ethnicity: Theory and Experience,
            Cambridge, Mass.: Harvard University
            Press. Pp. 305-349.

1978   "Migration in Caribbean Societies:
            Socio-economic and Symbolic
            Resource," In, W.H. McNeill & R.S.
            Adams (eds.), Human Migration:
            Patterns and Policies. Bloomington,
            Indiana: Indiana University Press,
            Pp. 106-145.

Petras, Elizabeth McLean
1981   "The Global Labor Market in the
            Modern World-Economy," In, M. Kritz,
            C.B. Keely & S. Tomasi (eds.).
            Global Trends in Migration: Theory
            and Research on International
            Population Movements. New York:
            Center for Migration Studies, Pp. 44-
            63.

Portes, Alejandro
1981   "Modes of Structural Incorporation
            and Present Theories of Labor
            Immigration," In, M. Kritz, C.B.
            Keely & S. Tomasi (eds.), Global
            Trends in Migration: Theory and
            Research on International Population
            Movements.   New York: Center for
            Migration Studies, Pp. 279-297.

Portes, Alejandro and John Walton
1981   Labor, Class and the International
            System. New York: Academic Press.

Redfield, Robert
    1947   "The Folk Society." American Journal
            of Sociology, Vol. 52: 293-308.

Redfield, Robert, Ralph Linton & Melville
Herskovits
    1936   "Memorandum for the Study of
            Acculturation." American
            Anthropologist, Vol. 38: 149-152.

Reid, Ira De Augustine
    1968 (1939)   The Negro Immigrant: His
            Background, Characteristics and
            Social Adjustment 1899-1937.
            New York: AMS Press.

Richardson, Bonham
    1983   Caribbean Migrants: Environment and
            Human Survival on St. Kitts and
            Nevis.   Knoxville: University of
            Tennessee Press.

Richmond, Anthony H.
    1981   "Immigrant Adaptation in a Post-
            Industrial Society," In, M. Kritz,
            C.B. Keely & S. Tomasi (eds.), Global
            Trends in Migration: Theory and
            Research on International Population
            Movements. New York: Center for
            Migration Studies, Pp. 298-319.

Ross, Marc H. and Thomas Weisner
    1977   "The Rural-Urban Migrant Network in
            Kenya: Some General Implications."
            American Ethnologist, Vol. 4(2): 359-
            375.

Rubenstein, Hymie
    1983   "Remittances and Rural
            Underdevelopment in the English-
            Speaking Caribbean." Human
            Organization, Vol. 42(4): 295-306.

Rubin, Vera and Marisa Zavalloni
1969   We Wish to be Looked Upon. New York: Teachers College Press, Columbia University.

Ryan, Selwyn D.
1972   Race and Nationalism in Trinidad and Tobago. Toronto: University of Toronto Press.

Sassen-Koob, Saskia
1981   "Towards a Conceptualization of Immigrant Labor," Social Problems, Vol. 29(1): 65-81.

Smith, M.G.
1965   "The Plural Framework of Jamaican Society," In, The Plural Society in the British West Indies. Berkeley: University of California Press, Pp. 162-175.

Sparrow, The Mighty
1968   "Mas' In Brooklyn," In, More Sparrow More. Trinidad, West Indies: RA Records.

Stack, Carol
1974   All Our Kin: Strategies for Survival in a Black Community. New York: Harper & Row.

Steinberg, Stephen
1981   The Ethnic Myth: Race, Ethnicity and Class in America. Atheneum Press.

Sutton, Constance and Susan Makiesky
1975   "Migration and West Indian Racial and Ethnic Consciousness," In, H. Safa & B. DuToit (eds.), Migration and Development. The Hague: Mouton Publishers, Pp. 113-144.

Szapocznik, Jose and William Kurtines
  1980   "Acculturation, Biculturalism and
            Adjustment Among Cuban Americans,"
            In, A. Padilla (ed.), Acculturation:
            Theory, Models and Some New Findings.
            Boulder, Colorado: Westview Press,
            Pp. 139-159.

Time Magazine
  1983   "The New Ellis Island." June 13, Pp.
            18-25.

United States Census
  1980   Bureau of the Census 20th, 1980
            Population, Ancestry of Population by
            State 1980.

United States Department of Justice
  1980   Immigration and Naturalization
            Service, Annual Reports, 1980.

van den Berghe, Pierre
  1981   The Ethnic Phenomenon. New York:
            Elsevier.

Watson, Hilbourne A.
  1976   "International Migration and the
            Political Economy of
            Underdevelopment: Aspects of the
            Commonwealth Caribbean Situation,"
            In, R. Bryce-Laporte & D. Mortimer
            (eds.). Caribbean Immigration to the
            United States. Washington, D.C.:
            Research Institute on Immigration and
            Ethnic Studies, Smithsonian
            Institution, Pp. 16-42.

Whitten, Norman, Jr. and Alvin Wolfe
  1973   "Network Analysis," In, John
            Honigmann (ed.), Handbook of Social
            and Cultural Anthropology. Chicago:
            Rand McNally & Co., Pp. 717-746.

Williams, Eric
    1969   Inward Hunger: The Education of a
                Prime Minister.   London: Andre
                Deutsch.

Wolf, Eric R.
    1966   "Kinship Friendship, and Patron-
                Client Relations in Complex
                Societies," In, M. Banton (ed.), The
                Social Anthropology of Complex
                Societies.   London: Tavistock
                Publications, Pp. 1-22.

INDEX

Acculturation, 10, 12, 14–15, 176, 182; process, 11

Adaptation, 68; of migrants, 4, 115; process, 104

American, 69, 140–142; Afro-, 181; Anglo-, 140–142, 146; black, 2, 6, 13, 18–19, 85, 170, 182, 183, 185; culture, 20; experience, 13; families, 69; legislation, 68; life, 4, 7, 155, 170, 183; minorities, 18, 155, 157, 159, 165, 183; racism, 17, 20, 150–153; scholarship, 2, social institution, 7; society, 3, 5, 6, 14, 16, 18, 19–22, 155, 181–183; white, 15, 33, 36, 85, 151, 154, 170, 183

Anti-Chinese Exclusion Act of 1882, 24, 72

Assimilation, 5–19, 47, 54, 176; barriers, 183, 185; goal, 5; lack of, 86; paradigm, 4, 5, 18, 182; racial, 16; structural, 13, 180–181; theory, 8

Association, 14, 81, 181; failure, 164; membership, 159; voluntary, 6, 158, 160–166, 171

Attitudes, 9, 10, 13, 15, 18, 20, 40

Barnes, J.A., 46

Beckford, George, 30, 31, 167

Behavior, 9, 15, 46, 47, 86, 174; dictatorial, 173; patterns, 104; symbolic, 158

Biculturalism, 11–12

Black, 36, 37, 154, 184; components, 6, 18; consciousness, 170, 185; family structure, 84; group, 17; women, 38, 124; worker, 54

Blauner, R., 8, 20, 183

Boissevain, J., 48, 92, 130, 131, 143

Boundaries, 48; componential, 181; geographical, 14, 100, 106; household, 100, 168; national, 4, 21, 116, 130, 177; racial/ethnic, 5; social-class, 150

Bott, Elizabeth, 46

Braveboy-Wagner, Jacqueline, 120

Braithwaite, L., 34, 167

Bryce-Laporte, Roy S., 1–3, 21–25

Caldwell, J. C., 121

Caribbean, 29, 35, 36, 41, 77, 170, 173, 177, 178, 185; Afro-, 3; Anglophone, 3, 36; bureaucracies, 117, 118; Commonwealth, 6, 23, 25, 167; connection, 156, 187; Economics, 23, 30, 167; employer, 31; English speaking, 3, 42, 151, 154, 186; migrant group, 72; political group, 165; population movement, 167; scholars, 38

Carnegie, C., 171, 172, 174

Choldin, H., 72

Class, 19; lower/middle/upper, 15, 33–35, 39–41, 121, 151;

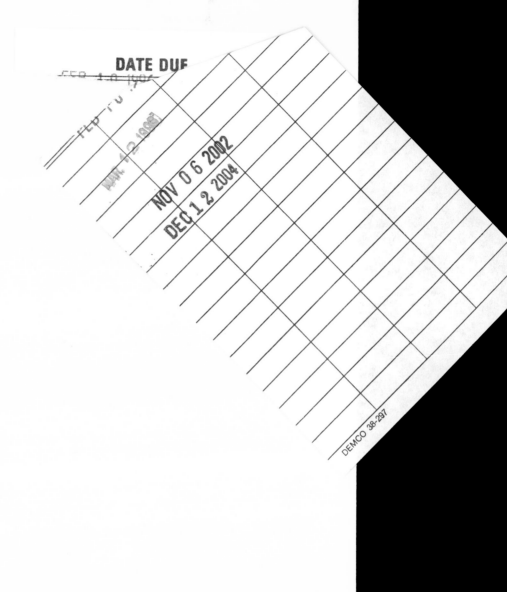